# The Four Archangels

# The Four Archangels

Angelic Inspiration for a
Balanced, Joyous Life

Michel Green

Copyright © 2010 by Michel Green.

Library of Congress Control Number: 2010917391
ISBN:          Hardcover      978-1-4568-2120-3
               Softcover      978-1-4568-2119-7
               Ebook          978-1-4568-2121-0

All rights reserved. The Four Archangels, the material contained herein and its original title, The Elemental Concepts of the Four Archangels, are the sole copyrighted property of Michel Green, and may not be reproduced by any means, electric, electronic, digital or otherwise available whether at the current time or developed at any time in the future without the express prior written consent of the channel and author.

This book was printed in the United States of America.

Contact with Mrs Green may be made by writing to
Box 213 Evergreen Park NW, Edmonton, AB T5Y 4M2 Canada

By e-mail to veiledmoon@shaw.ca

Or through her websites: *www.veiledmoon.com*
*www.metaphysicianmichel.com* [The Wisdom Keeper's Way]

**To order additional copies of this book, contact:**
Xlibris Corporation
1-888-795-4274
www.Xlibris.com
Orders@Xlibris.com
90044

# Contents

Gratitude ......................................................................................................... 7
Acknowledgements ........................................................................................ 9
The Four Archangels ..................................................................................... 11

Chapter I: Acceptance ................................................................................... 15
    From the Mind of the Archangel Gabriel ................................................ 17
    Through the Healing of the Archangel Raphael ...................................... 23
    With the Inspiration of the Archangel Uriel ............................................ 27
    With the Love of the Archangel Michael ................................................ 32

Chapter II: Forgiveness .................................................................................. 36
    A Factor of the Mind—Archangel Gabriel ............................................. 38
    A Feeling of the Heart—Archangel Raphael .......................................... 45
    The Inspiring Spirit—Archangel Uriel ................................................... 51
    The Practical Practise—Archangel Michael ............................................ 57

Chapter III: Celebration ................................................................................ 63
    Talk to Your Heart—Archangel Gabriel .................................................. 65
    Heal through Celebration—Archangel Raphael ..................................... 70
    Celebrating All Life Everywhere—Metatron .......................................... 75
    Celebrate the Unity—Archangel Michael ............................................... 79

Chapter IV: Commencement ........................................................................ 85
    Thought Begins It—Archangel Gabriel .................................................. 87
    Feeling your Way—Archangel Raphael .................................................. 95
    The Gestation of Peace—Metatron ........................................................ 99
    The W/Holistic Journey—Archangel Michael ....................................... 106

Chapter V: Courage ....................................................................................... 114
    Courage is of the Heart—Archangel Gabriel .......................................... 116
    No Strings Attached—Archangel Raphael ............................................. 124
    The Soul's Courage—Archangel Uriel ................................................... 129

    Courage and Choice—Archangel Michael ................................................ 135

Chapter VI: Deserving ............................................................................. 140
    Self-Worth—Archangel Gabriel ............................................................ 142
    Self-Healing—Archangel Raphael ......................................................... 149
    Self-Empowerment—Archangel Uriel .................................................. 152
    Self-Value—Archangel Michael .............................................................. 157

Chapter VII: Uniqueness ......................................................................... 162
    The Box is a Trap—Archangel Gabriel ................................................. 164
    The Walls are Insecure—Archangel Raphael ........................................ 169
    The View is Unexpected—Archangel Uriel .......................................... 172
    I AM Choice—Archangel Michael ........................................................ 178

Chapter VIII: Exploration ....................................................................... 183
    The Journey of Inspiration—Archangel Gabriel .................................. 184
    The Journey of Intuition—Archangel Raphael .................................... 190
    The Journey of Consultation—Archangel Uriel .................................. 195
    The Search for Peace—Archangel Michael .......................................... 201

Questions and Answers ........................................................................... 207

# GRATITUDE

I am continually Blessed to be
The Channel of the Archangel Michael
Bringing his Loving Wisdom and Guidance to each of you

I am continually Appreciative and De-Lighted by those who have been my
 audiences and my students
I am continually Grateful to God, Goddess, All That Is
for my Life and the learning and love it brings

I am continually warmed and supported
By my Beloved Dave
My children: Sandi and Evan,
And my Grandsons: Jordan, Cody and Travis

In humility,
May the Wonder and Joy that I have been given be reflected in a Wonder-full
 and Joy-filled Life of your own

# ACKNOWLEDGEMENTS

I wish to sincerely acknowledge and thank Jason Land. The work of transcribing the uplifting words of the Archangels was done by Jason using voice recognition technology in his own unique manner to ensure its accuracy. I am also grateful to Jason for the many hours of basic formatting done on the material. I know well it is no mean feat to make grammatical sense of the complex and involved "sentences" used by these Higher Beings. His help has been of major assistance in the production of this work.

I also wish to thank Jeremy Umerez, Amy Ramirez and Rey August of Xlibris Publishing for their assistance, guidance and support during the publication of "The Four Archangels." Their courtesy and generosity with their knowledge is appreciated.

Most of all, I wish to express my Joy and Gratitude for the Faith, Grace and loving support of the Archangels who, as the Archangel Michael promised more than 20 years, have always answered the call. Their agreement to participate in this project when it first began as a lecture series was not only magnificently fulfilled, but their encouragement and guidance to bring that information into book format has been steadfast and enthusiastic—and I have been utterly caught up in that vibration. Their excitement and confidence is encouraging as always. I hope you catch it too!

Bright Blessings,
Michel Green
Edmonton, Alberta, Canada
14 November 2010

# THE FOUR ARCHANGELS

### Angelic Inspiration for a Balanced, Joyous Life

The Archangel Michael spoke. *"Let us,"* he said, *"gather with our Dear Brethren and share our Divine inspiration with Humanity that they may also be inspired to bring balance and Joy into their Life experiences."*

I personally was not sure; however, I implicitly trust the Archangel Michael. When he indicated that I was ready to channel the energetic wisdom and Love of four different Archangels in a single evening, I accepted the Truth of his statement.

And this was the beginning of an amazing eight-part series of talks based on words of encouragement and empowerment. At each gathering, I was honoured to carry the energy, wisdom and knowledge of the Archangels speaking on the same topic. The Archangel Michael was a speaker at all the sessions as were the Archangels Gabriel and Raphael. On other occasions, Metatron alternated with the Archangel Uriel.

The talks were designed to focus on the evening's key word through the use of the four ancient elements of Air [thought], Water [emotion], Fire [inspiration] and Earth [physicality or practicality]. In this way, a w/holistic view of the theme was developed.

Let me briefly introduce you to our Speakers:

## Archangel Michael

Protector and Guide, champion of All Life Everywhere, Captain of the Army of the Lord and Head of the Angelic Forces on the planet at this time, the Archangel Michael is a laughter-loving, practical and compassionate leader who speaks on behalf of the Most High in an encouraging, up-lifting way bringing messages of support and Love from the One he calls the Beloved Divine. The Archangel Michael is known, beloved and honoured by three of the world's major religions: Jewish, Muslin and Christian. Many spiritually inclined people feel a strong relationship to this Champion of the Light. Acknowledged as the Great Prince, Archangel Michael is celebrated at several feast days particularly November 21 and September 29 [Michaelmas].

## Archangel Gabriel

The Archangel Gabriel is one of the few archangels who regularly appears in varying forms—some experience Gabriel as female, others as male. Gabriel is the Archangel most concerned with communication and carrying important messages from God to specially chosen individuals. He brought the word to Elizabeth and Zaccariah that they would have a son to be named John and then carried a similar but much more significant message to Elizabeth's cousin, Mary, about the conception and impending birth of her son, Jesus. Gabriel is also renowned for dictating the words of the Holy Quran to Mohammed. Gabriel speaks with a resounding sound that is intended to capture the attention of the audience and impress the importance of the Divine words that are being conveyed. Archangel Gabriel's feast day is March 24. If you need help with speaking to anyone, simply ask the Archangel Gabriel to "guide my words."

## Archangel Raphael

This is the Archangel of Divine Healing; gentle, compassionate, filled with the wisdom of healing methodologies and what also could be called a Grandmother's healing knowledge. He often shares the origins of imbalanced experiences and discusses what needs to be cleared from this lifetime or another to facilitate healing in every level, every body and every dimension. Archangel Raphael's gentle manner is like a velvet glove that covers a strength, determination and faith that All Will Be Well until it is. Archangel Raphael's feast day is celebrated on October 24.

## Archangel Uriel

The Archangel Uriel is known as the Great Archangel of the Earth being the keeper of the mysteries of the planet, and the guide and protector of the Nature Spirits and their work. Archangel Uriel is called the Light or Fire of God and, thus can be very inspiring. His feast day is celebrated July 28. Archangel Uriel is strong and can be somewhat stern is requiring us to live up to our potential while still understanding the need for kindness. He is a very Joy-full Being who brings enthusiasm, vitality and dynamic eagerness for a life of bliss and wonder. Many of the highest initiatory teachings are guided by Archangel Uriel.

## Metatron

Like his twin brother, Sandalphon, Metatron has lived the life of an incarnated human—the only two in the Angelic Realm to have done so. In his human life, Metatron was known as the prophet Enoch, a scribe and leader of his people. Metatron now is the Recorder or Scribe of the Most High as well as being the Over-seer of the Akashic Records. He has been honoured with the gift of being able to sit in the presence of God. He has a special concern for children and education. The feast day of Metatron is October 1.

Following the talks, the Archangel Michael responded to questions from the audience. Those questions and answers of greatest relevance to a general audience have been included in the final section of this book.

# CHAPTER I

# Acceptance

A rchangels Gabriel, Raphael, Uriel, and Michael focussed on speaking from the mental concept of Acceptance, as well as the practical advantages of Acceptance, to the emotional and inspirational ways of bringing Acceptance into a balanced practice in one's Life.

In the Mind of the Archangel Gabriel, encouragement is given to accepting the bounty of The Divine as a Gift for creating Joy in all things.

The Archangel Raphael shares a healing meditation as part of his talk.

Uriel the Archangel speaks of risk and trust as part of accepting—the use of Free Will in Life's expressions.

Love, pure and simple, is the central point of the Archangel Michael's presentation.

The Angels remind us that by being open to accepting the gifts that Life offers we can also be open to the benefits and joyousness of Life. By accepting that all our experiences are intended to lead us to positiveness, we shift our results as well.

# From the Mind of the Archangel Gabriel

Wonderful Ones, it is with great pleasure that we accept and are very delighted at this opportunity of bringing our messages to your ears in this new and exciting format—Four of us speaking our hearts and our love, our encouragement, our support, to you, indeed.

We have come to encourage within you the practice of Acceptance; in some cases the practice of Acceptance as it is and in other cases the practice of Acceptance as your strength, as your possibility, as your potential, to create that which can be.

My Loves, Wonderful, Wonderful Ones, when we say, Acceptance, we are encouraging you to look at the circumstances in your life, and decide for yourself—is any one circumstance, is any one event, is any one condition, acceptable to you?

For I say to you that when you accept and say, "This condition is difficult. This condition is traumatic. This condition hurts me, but I will accept it because this is what God wants for me;"

When you say, "I have faith, and I will not question it;"

When you say, "I follow the dictates of my religion or my spiritual belief as it is, and I will not investigate it," that is blind faith, Wonderful Ones, and the God of Your Understanding wants you to look at your circumstances, to look at the conditions that are around you, to be open-eyed, clear, and aware of what is happening there, and then decide—is it acceptable to you?

Can you agree with it?

Can you accept it as what a benevolent, loving God would choose for you?

You must understand, very clearly—all of the circumstances that occur to you in your life have been chosen by you, for the growth of your life, but if you sit there and say, "The world can bash me, and I will only say, 'This is what God wants for me. I have faith in God, and I will not question it, and I will not question the circumstances.'" that is blind faith; but, what we encourage of you is a dynamic, interactive, evolving faith, a faith that questions every attribute; so that you can come to a deeper, richer understanding; so that you can transcend those circumstances that cause you pain, that cause you imbalance, that push you out of harmony, that say to you, "This doesn't feel to me like a loving God."

We want you to go beyond that.

Now then, you say, "How can I accept the circumstances, how can I accept my faith and still question it?"

What we desire for you, what we are calling you to, is a conscious life, a life of partnership with The Divine, not someone who stands there with their begging-bowl and says, "Hand me whatever leftovers you want; obviously, I don't deserve much if you are not going to give me much." But rather like the child in the Dickens's story:

When you accept that you have influence,

That you have free will,

That you have a responsibility, as a co-creator of your Life, as an equal partner with The Divine—

When you say, "Please God, I want more," it's not saying, "I want more of this thin, meagre gruel that you first handed out to me," but

> I want more. I want a richer life. I want a more abundant life. I hold my hands out to accept all the good that you can give me, all the joy, all the riches, all the abundance of friendships, all the conditions and circumstances that will benefit me, and yes, I understand that life is like a cycle . . . and at some times things work well and other times things do not work well . . . and I accept that everything is changing; therefore, I will not hold myself in a circumstance that involves self-denigration, and poverty, and despair, and imbalance, and lack, because that is what God would have me go beyond. When I accept God as my partner, I am accepting all the circumstances that that Partner would have for me. When I hang around with people who have a rich, abundant point of view in their lives, I am putting myself in that vibration; therefore, I am coming to accept that that vibration is in harmony within me as well.

When you hang around with The Divine as your partner, as your Creator—but one who creates out of Himself, not one who creates less than Herself—"When I accept The Divine as my partner, as my supportive, loving Guide, then Life works for me, infinitely better than it works when I am by myself, because I have now just joined forces with The Infinite," but you do not accept.

You sit in your circumstances, and you moan them, or you disparage them, or you say to yourself, "This is not what I wanted," and some of you struggle to go beyond where you are, and some of you carry a great burden, feeling that that burden is yours and yours alone, but when you accept all the good that can occur in your life, Dear and Glorious, Wonderful Ones, please, please, do accept—

First of all, primarily, it is important that you accept The Divine, accept that Great Being, as your greatest ally, your most formidable lover, your most enthusiastic supporter—when you accept that The Divine has your best interests at heart, that The Divine desires for you all goodness, then your life can certainly be changed.

But when you continue to accept societal agreements and old, old, old, imperfect teachings, slave teachings, keep-the-people-in-their-place teachings, power-filled teachings, that say, "You don't deserve—to know this, to have this, to participate in this;" that say to you, "You must work hard for everything that you have;" that say to you, "You're on your own. Nobody cares."

When you accept The Divine, giving all your worries and all your problems to The Divine, when you say, "This is my plate, and it is filled to overflowing, and I cannot handle it all; I'm just at the end of my string. I cannot handle it all,"—then don't.

You were never intended to, and why do you have more, and more, and more, and more things piled up on you?—to give you the strength, to give you the determination, to give you the ability, to say:

> I can't do this alone. Here God, I'll look after these three square inches, and You can have everything else. You can look after my relationships. You can look after my finances. You can look after my friendships. I'm going to focus on what I can do in this circumstance, and there are days when all I can do is drag myself from the bed to the living room, to the chair in the living room, and just sit there and hold on to my life, and there are other days, forgive me if I feel that I am capable of handling the entire world and all of its problems, and I understand truly that I cannot, but I feel so empowered, and I know that is a gift from You. I accept that energy and that gift from You, but, in the meantime, please look after this. I accept, and I trust, and I have faith, that You will, indeed, look after me in a manner far, far richer, and far, far nobler, and far, far more abundantly and lovingly, than I will look after myself.

And those of you who have heard some of this before, we will say to you—

> Do not check up on The Divine. Have the faith that says, 'In Divine right time, for my Highest Good, for my Greatest Joy, all will be looked after, and, in the meantime, I will do what I can in each circumstance from a point of view of serenity because when I give my problems to The

Divine, all the worries that I have wrapped those problems in, go with it. I don't have them anymore. I'm not going to hold them anymore. I'm not going to believe in those worries anymore. I am going to accept that The Divine is looking after me, and; therefore, I can work on accepting the second part of my Life circumstance which is accepting that I am here to live an abundantly, joyful life. I am going to change my thought patterns and only accept—in my thoughts and in my speech and in my connection with every other life form—I am going to accept that I am a worthy, deserving, serene individual who has no necessity—really—to engage in fear, no necessity in any way, shape, or form to engage in criticism, in lack, in feeling that I do not deserve or that I only deserve that which hinders me, that which hurts me, but rather I am saying that I deserve, and I am open to receiving—I happily accept—every delight that is available, and I don't do it from a point of desperation.

Those of you who get engaged in prosperity work, initially come to that through a form of desperation, and that desperation, that crossing your fingers and "squinching" your face up and hoping that this will work, interferes with the process, but when you accept—accept yourself as a Child of The Divine, accept the fact that the loving God has a great interest in your fulfilling yourself at the highest degree—when you accept that you are worthy of all the radiant, joyful experiences of Life, and you accept it from a state of calm and centeredness, then you become exceedingly powerful, then you become in such a state where magic works [at least to those who are not there it almost seems like magic], or like great, good luck—a luck that you have created yourself through your own faith, through accepting your worthiness, through accepting the goodness that you can have in your life, through accepting the thoughts that lead to the feelings that Life is a bountiful, beneficial, delightful place/experience.

You are here to transcend any and all experiences you judge to be negative. You are here to accept that they are here for your work, for your blessing, to give you an experience that is amazingly uplifting. And, when you understand that: going beyond the fears—rather than accepting the circumstances, "Hey, this is what God wants for me."

No, that is not what God wants for you—you have chosen that experience in order to go beyond it. You have chosen that experience in order to move away from it. Those of you who say, "Life . . . my life is not abundant," need to go out into your gardens and measure out a square-foot of grass and count all the blades of grass; need to look at the circumstances in New Orleans where there was great devastation, and that devastation was created by agreement, by all the Souls living there, to change their circumstances, so that they could move beyond the negative energy that had built itself up, and so they could accept—by being open to accepting, by being open to receiving—they could accept the goodness of the world. And every individual who has sent a dollar, a blessing, a bus, anything that has been there, anyone who has sent to that place a thought of, 'How terrible, I wish I could help,' anyone who has sent any form of healing energy, has been part of that process, part of that karma—to let these people know that they are worthy of better than they had. And so miracles have happened and continue to happen.

Every circumstance in your life is there to give you an opportunity to expand it if it is already good or to change it if it is not what you desire.

Every single circumstance in your life is to be accepted as the gift that it is, for your growth, but it is not to be accepted without the responsibility of doing something with it, whether you receive it and say, "This suits me exactly as it is," or whether you accept it and say, "This is for my growth." And with all growth change is involved, and some of it you will say . . .

> God, I know You gave this to me so that I could learn something. Well, what I've learned is that I don't want this particular form, and so I give this worry back to You. I give this problem back to You. You solve it, and let me know when You're done, and I accept that I have that Free Will. I have that choice. I can say to You, 'I trust You to look after it better than I can look after it, and I don't have to worry about it.'

. . . And this is what we mean by living a conscious life—by looking at every single circumstance daily, even hourly, as it comes to your attention,

> Is this for my greatest joy? Not as it is . . . then what do I need to do, as a conscious, aware representative of Divine Love, to make this more of a statement of that Love, and if it already is a form of Amazing Love, what can I do to expand it, enhance it, share it with others, radiate it?

This is living life consciously. This is accepting that your circumstances are there for your benefit.

In some instances, circumstances come into your life so that you can be a channel for benefit to others, but, as our Channel will tell you, every time you send something out into the world to benefit others, you, as the conduit or the channel or the representative of Divine Love, also receive a benefit of Love, provided you are willing to accept it.

Wonderful Ones, there are many of you who have a great capacity for saying, "I will accept this into my life because then I can give it away," and that's fine. That is laudable, but we will say to you that that is not the ultimate goal because every circumstance that occurs in your Life is for you. What you do with it is secondary.

What you do with it is a representation of how you have grown and evolved, but if you feel that you can manipulate or make conditions with The Universe by saying, "I will accept this so that I can do something for somebody else," then you may not get it because that is saying, "I'm not worthy to have it or handle it," and so it is deeply important that you accept yourselves as worthy, and you can only do that by accepting yourselves as Children of The Divine, blessed with all that The Divine is capable of.

So it is our challenge to you, Dear and Wonderful Ones. When you accept The Divine wholly as a Perfected Being—rich, loving, gracious, generous, delighted in all of your joys, laughing with all of your laughter, hopeful with all of your dreams and hopes—when you accept that, and create yourself in that Image, then you are truly accepting yourself as Divine, as a continuation of The Divine, as a co-creator with The Divine; then you are truly accepting all the gifts that are being offered to you. We await your response.

# Through the Healing of the Archangel Raphael

Beautiful Beings, I would ask you to join in a meditation and accept the healing that is possible, as you work with this vibration.

> Dear Hearts, allow yourselves to envision around you the Circle of Your Guides and Guardians, and around this circle see and know a beautiful band of dark, blue Light, moving from right to left around your circle. As this Light moves around the circle, it expands and grows . . . down into the floor, up and over your circle like a protective dome.
>
> See and know, within the centre of your circle, a flowing energy of pale-blue Light, moving from left to right in front of you, and as you watch this pale blueness, see and know it to be filled with pale, puffy, white clouds, a beautiful, radiant energy that moves into the heart centre of each of you in your circle. As you continue with the blue Lights, moving in opposite directions behind you and in front of you, allow and accept that you are coming into a state of great harmony, alignment, and balance . . .
>
> Now, moving down from the top of the dome, see and know an iridescent beam of incredible, beautiful, White Light—coming down from the top of the dome to the floor in front of you and through it. As you watch, this beam of White Light grows larger and larger until it is a pillar of magnificent, soothing, healing, White energy. Allow yourself to move gently into this pillar and feel the peace, the relaxation, and the healing comfort of being in Divine Presence. Accept it as holy, as you are able . . .
>
> Now, invite those who have meaning for you, those individuals whose names come to your attention—whether you would expect them to or not—invite them into the Healing Light, and allow them to stay or leave, as they choose . . .
>
> With healing, accept Divine Love . . . Accept Bliss . . .

I am here to encourage you to accept all the various forms of healing and emotional abundance that we can deliver to you. Many of you, being involved in your worldly affairs, have also accepted the conditions of this world which includes accelerated levels of stress, and the resulting imbalances in your lives are causing chaos within the cells of the body, are causing conditions that, in their manifestation, bring messages to you.

When you accept that your life is to be a journey of Joy,

When you accept that your body is a temple of Divinity,

When you accept that you have emotional states in order that you can pray more effectively and choose those emotional states that are healing, life-enhancing, and worshipful for you,

Then you will find the conditions of your life becoming more and more a positive statement of how Life can best be lived rather than a panic-stricken, stress-filled experience.

We know that there are circumstances going on in the world where there are infusions of energy. Since November of 2002, there have been regular influxes or influences of different types of intense energy. Many individuals on the planet have striven to balance the negative energies that have come in and to erase from their lives those results. Many of you have or are taking steps toward what would be a more contented Life. Others of you are still dealing with the chaos and the uncertainty of life as it is, while dreaming and feeling in your heart that there must be more to Life than this, that often you feel or you say to yourself, "Is this all there is?"

And of course the answer is no.

What you see around you is the lesser part of All That Is, but until you heal your vision, until you reorient your way of looking at the world, until you turn yourself upside down so that you can have a different point of view, your tendency is to continue as you have always done, allowing the beliefs, the values, the statements, the understandings, the agreements of society, to run your life for you.

I say to you that when you accept responsibility for what occurs in your Life, when you say . . .

> My heart is broken at these circumstances. I know I cannot ignore them. I know I can no longer put on rose-coloured glasses and say, 'That is the other side of the world. It does not apply to me,' but I feel in my heart that I must do something, that I must pray, or I must work, or I must be of service, or must indeed move forward, make a difference, be a change—

When you come to that point, then indeed you are beginning to live and to accept the wholeness of your purpose. I have given the message before that **HEAL** means to "**H**elp **E**veryone **A**ttain **L**ove", and so it is.

And you say, "But my life is so busy, how can I find the time for one more thing to do?" And we say to you 'As you heal yourself, as you treat yourself with greater Love, as you relinquish those circumstances that are not life-enhancing, you will have the time. You will have the inspiration, and you will come to understand what it is that you could do.'

By allowing yourself the opportunity to heal your Life—to look at every segment of your life and say, "This is something I would work on. This is something I could release. This is something I could let go of. This is something I can change and make more beautiful, more loving, more healed"—then you are accepting that the Love you came here to radiate, the Love that you came here to emanate and share with every Being, for their healing and yours, is indeed the most valued work that you can do.

As many of you are aware, there are a great many programs on your television about clearing clutter and creating beautiful, functional, even one might say, healed and healing spaces for individuals, and this is a symbol of the state of life as it is—chaotic—as it could be—serene, beautiful, effective, and a delight to be in. All of those are components of a Healing Life.

Each and every one of you has the vibration of a healer, and whether your intention is to work specifically with healing yourselves or being of service to others and offering healing to them is immaterial because you are Beings of Energy, and you cannot radiate, or perform, or accept into your life, healed energy, the energy of self-respect, the energy of Love, the energy of upliftment—you cannot accept that into your life, into your physical self, into your circumstances—without it reaching out and touching many others.

By accepting your gifts as a healer, by accepting your understanding that everything you do or do not do has one of two effects: to make your life, the life of All Lives Everywhere, the life of the world, better; or to detract from that betterment. As Gabriel has said, "This is again a call for a conscious life."

When you intend to use the abilities that you have, the consciousness that you have, for the betterment of self and others, you are accepting your role of a love-radiator, a love-giver, and that is, in essence, the reason that you are here—is to work with that energy. When you understand and take that understanding out of your mind and put it in your heart so that it becomes emotionally a part of who you are, so that you radiate it with Joy, so that you fill your Life, every corner, every nook, every cranny, with the sunshine of your Joy, then you light up the lives of many, many others around you—some of whom you will never even know because that radiance that you have sent off has touched the spark in another heart and set in motion a radiance that has been accepted there, and it too moves out into the world and touches other hearts.

It is very much like many of the candles that the Dalai Lama has blessed, and having blessed them and distributed them, these candles go out into the world and light other candles, carrying with it that loving radiance, that acceptance that life can be a little better because he shines his Light, and he brings to other people the awareness of their light, and so the candle comes from the Dalai Lama to one and lights many other candles, taking that radiance with it, and each of those candles lights many other candles, taking the radiance again, and you have fifth and sixth and twelfth and twentieth generations of candles, we might say. All of them carrying the blessings of Peace, Joy, and Love, infused into these lights by the original candles blessed by the Dalai Lama.

Each of you is like one of those blessed candles, and each of you has the ability to share that onward from you, in circle after circle of Radiant Love, and as that Love goes forward and is accepted by others, taken into their hearts to ponder, it begins to pulsate and radiate from them. And so, Love and Healing are accepted around the world, and I remind you that it is not about Loving and Healing only the human race in the world.

It is about blessing and sending healing energy to the ground on which wars have been held, that they might stabilize, that they might come to grow in beauty.

It is by sending out healing energy to the animals who are under threat, the animals who are companions in your Life, the animals who still run wild and free, and allowing them to be bathed in your concern and your consideration, and it is sending healing energy to and through the crystal partners that are also part of the life forms of this planet.

By participating in this manner with All Life Everywhere, the planet herself and life elsewhere, you join forces with the Tibetans who long ago accepted themselves, along with other groups, to be the Guardians of the Wisdom of The Divine and to share that and keep it safe and keep it sacred for the knowledge and the understanding of those to come after. Many Tibetans meditate regularly, and those who follow Tibetan patterns also do so—meditate regularly for the healing, the upliftment, the support, the encouragement of All Life Everywhere. Consider that this planet is only one small grain in a vast sea, and then you will understand the scope of the work that they do.

As you accept yourself as a valued member of the healing agents, you will understand that your role is also to be part of the healing of All Life Everywhere. For those who were included in your meditation, we have taken note, and with your permission, I will send those of my healing forces to be with them, to encourage them, to let them know of your love and ours as well. We recommend this meditation as part of your regular practice. It allows you to stabilize and assist the world in general.

Accept our blessings, Dear Hearts, and we will continue to have them flow to you.

# With the Inspiration of the Archangel Uriel

Dear and Glorious, Wonderful Beings of Light, how delightful to see you from this perspective. Ever and always, we have seen the Soul energy of who you are, and now we see through the Channel's eyes how beautiful, how radiant, how diverse.

How sad that you do not accept yourselves as the magnificent creatures that we know you to be. We are grateful for this time and this opportunity, and we will say to you that many of you say, "Why should I accept the difficulties in my life. I don't like them. They're not enough fun," and this we would agree.

They are there for your learning.

They are there to make you stronger.

They are there to inspire you to go beyond the boundaries that they would create around you.

They are not there for permanence.

They are not there to run your lives.

They are not there for you to be held bound as a prisoner.

They are there for a purpose, and having obtained that purpose, to be released, to be let go of;

So that you can go on to the reward that follows;

So that you can move yourselves into a bright and beautiful time of your lives;

So that you can learn how to stretch that positive vibration and how to help it expand, help it strengthen you through laughter as well as through the testing.

Like a sword going into the fire, it is tempered and tested and strengthened, but it does not stay there forever, or it becomes weak. It must be brought out and put into the coolness of the water and become strong. And so this is what your life is meant to be—cycles, and cycles, and cycles, of change, of being tested, of being tempered, of dealing with issues that may be difficult. But if you look at them as a way of advancing who you are, and what you can be, and how you can be allowing yourself to be more and brighter and more beautiful, more finely attuned, more firmly shaped, then you will see that this cycle of negativity strengthens you, allows you to be shaped into a beautiful, finely-honed shape, and then you can go out and do that which you came to do, as an instrument—perhaps as an instrument in the hand of a Divine Surgeon that cuts away that which is not life-enhancing to a body so that beauty can then result and helpfulness can then result.

But I say that sadly we see often you do not even accept The Good in your lives. Many of you practice over and over to be so solemn. It is a wonder your face muscles do not ache to smile, and laugh, and release, and learn. For when you experience Life and you laugh as you do so, it becomes much easier to learn the lesson. It is a sadness to us and at times, we admit, a puzzlement that the Joys in your life do not seem to touch you as deeply as the sad-nesses in your life. They do not stay with you. They are not felt as intensely. You do not accept the wonderfulness about yourselves.

If you could see you as we see you, would you love yourselves more?

You are to be encouraged to love yourselves, to accept yourselves as you are. Many of you have stresses about the physical body, or what you feel capable of or incapable of. Many of you stress about your abilities to do what you would love to do, and all that is necessary to know is if it brings you Joy, then it is doing what its purpose is. Many of you put yourselves through the rack by being in work that is a torture to do, a challenge to drag yourself to, and then you wonder why you are not happy in your lives—because you have blocked off this little voice inside you that says, 'Do this, do this, do this. Yeah, I know there's money over there, but come over here, and do this, do this, do this.'

As you accept that which makes you happiest, everything else falls into place. It truly does; because, when you fill yourself with the happiness of what you can accomplish, when you fill yourself with the delight of doing what makes you feel so good, all positive energies come to that: abundance comes to that, because you are radiating Joy. It is a very attractive energy, and it will bring to it that which is in harmony or resonance to it.

My Dearest Hearts, we strongly wish to inspire you to give yourself the chance. Yes—it is true—accepting that which your heart desires—impossible though it may seem that it could support you—accepting that, and doing that, and having the intention that that will be what you desire to have, that it will support you, that it will be an inspirational and wonderful event in your life, it cannot be a single event. It pulls everything else to it.

The happier you are at what you do, the more people are attracted to that happiness, the more they say, "That person is having so much fun. I need to go over there to see what's going on," and so they do, and some will say, 'Well, they're just having way too much fun over there. I mean really.' Well, maybe you are having way too much fun over there. How wonderful is that, indeed?

My Dearest Loves, it is so much that we would encourage you. You criticize your physical selves, but know that your physical self, as it is now, is what got you to where you are. There must have been some value in it. You say to yourself, "Well, I'm not this, or I'm not that, or I'm not something else." No, perhaps not, but you are a Child of The Divine. You are a radiantly lovely Being.

I say to you, "If you could see yourselves as we see you, you would know and discover that you are amazingly beautiful, amazingly dynamic, amazingly effective, in all that you do." It is a risk.

It is a risk—it is true—to open up to that. Some people will say, 'Well, she's really full of herself isn't she?' But the fact of the matter is . . . Of course you are. Why would you not be full of who you are, when you are an emanation of Divine Love, Divine Joy? It bubbles up inside of you if you give it the chance to be expressed. My Loves, we encourage you to take that risk, trusting that The Divine will take care of you if you follow what keeps coming up for you.

That is when you put Acceptance of Divine Will as your first priority: as Gabriel said, "When you accept The Divine first, giving all your worries and all your problems over to The Divine and saying, 'I will do as I feel guided to do,' and just following that, trusting that everything will be looked after." I say to you, and the Channel will confirm to you, that that is a magical, magnificent place to be, and all the good that you desire will come to you, provided you stay in that state of calm acceptance.

That's the tricky part.

There are times when it would be very useful for you to be able to take your mind and dial up the thought of Acceptance, of all the abundance and all the joy and all the good in this world, and just weld it there, but you have Free Will, and you are allowed to change. Change, indeed, is the only constant that occurs on this plane. Taxes . . . There are places without taxes. Death . . . Even death is not decreed for every creature. There are instances in every single one of your Holy Books of individuals who have translated or gone directly from the physical realm into the world of The Divine without going through the death process, but change occurs, always.

And that is a very freeing thing. Every circumstance in your life that is not to your liking can be changed. Every circumstance in your life that you would do over can be changed. Every circumstance in your life that does not fulfill you can be changed. Even the cells in the body change on a regular basis—in something under a year, the entire physical body, except for a few white cells, is completely changed, and, of course, you know what that means to your partners. There is hope!

Indeed, My Loves, indeed, there is always hope. There is always the possibility, the potential. What would you choose to change? How would you allow yourself to grow? By allowing yourself to be inspired, by allowing yourself to go through the circumstances in your life—look into your past, to your childhood perhaps, or a few years ago—and saying, "Well, I once thought I'd like to try that, but I haven't gotten around to it, and yet it still keeps coming into my consciousness."

Well, give it a shot—give it three months, give it six months. If it starts a little bit, if you do it part time, if you do it once a week or once a month, and it's successful, allow it to build. Allow it to grow. Nurture it. Foster it. Encourage it. Have fun with it. That is what you are here to do. You are here to experience abundant, great Joy.

You're not here to experience war; although, some of you have, and some of you will, and whether it is a personal war with one other individual, or being in places like Iraq, war it is. And, some of you are here to experience ill health, and that too can change. Some of it can be avoided. Others of it, if you will listen before it becomes to the state where you must undergo an impact, then you don't have to experience the totality of certain circumstances, but always you will be given the opportunity to have magnificent lessons for your benefit.

Everything happens for a reason and a purpose—to serve you, not to irritate you, not to frustrate you, not to knock you to your knees as a control issue, not so you can experience a vengeful God, but so that you can go beyond where you are and come in to what you truly can be. Each of you has an amazing potential. Each of you has a heart filled to overflowing with love. In circumstances that aren't going well, when you desire to manifest something, and it doesn't happen, what that is saying is: "There wasn't enough desire there. There wasn't enough passion. There wasn't enough emotion there."

All prayer is, is a focused emotion; because, if we do not understand from you, if The Divine does not understand from you, that something is important enough for you to give your energy to, your love to, your focus to, then there is confusion. There is a slowing down, but when you allow yourself to be passionately involved with what you desire, then things can move, then you get what it is that you desire. It is important that you allow yourself to be inspired. On your public television services at this point in time there is a talk by our wonderful friend, Wayne Dyer, about living an inspired life. An Inspired Life is one that takes you outside of where you are and opens you up to possibilities and potentials, to create courage and the cycle of change that you may not have considered that you could possibly have.

Now, we are not saying that you need to undergo excruciating circumstances. What we are saying . . .

> Find something you love. Find something that is important to you. Find a star to hitch yourself to, and move with that, and work with that. However slow it might seem at first is immaterial. You have all heard of the power of a mustard seed, and if you would take a look at them, they are not terribly large. There are many seeds that are much larger, and yet that has the power to create something magnificent. So too do you with your greater intelligence, with your greater creativity, with your higher and more responsive connection to The Divine. You have a greater ability than the mustard seed to create exactly what you desire. It is only a matter of picking, from all the possibilities that you have what you'd like to start with. It's not necessary to have the perfect answer for your entire life. It is only necessary to have the answer for this moment, and so if today, working with a small child or painting, is what makes you feel satisfaction, then do it, and if it only lasts for three months, that's fine. You've had three months of enjoyment, of pleasure, of creativity, of great delight, and that can inspire you to go on to something else, something more, something brighter, something wonderful, and all it ever has to do is make you happy. When you accept that you are a creator and that you have the option and the opportunity to connect with Divine Inspiration—as long as you're having fun at it—that's the important thing. That's what's necessary. You are, each of you, a Radiance of Beautiful Light. The Light that you emanate in your consideration for yourselves and for others is an ongoing thing. Each of you has a particular vibration, a particular colour, a particular harmony, as in the singing of a magnificent chorus.

The word *Universe* itself means *One Song* and so all of Life is, indeed, one glorious song and only you can sing your part.

Sing, and laugh with the singing.

Sing, and enjoy the resonance within you because we will miss you, and we will miss your voice, if you choose not to sing, if you choose not to love, if you choose not to enjoy the life that you have.

Beloved Ones, we look to you to laugh much, and live your lives richly. Our blessings and our great delight in all that you do.

# With the Love of the Archangel Michael

Dearly Beloved, it is an exceptional evening, and we do appreciate your attention. All that has been said about Acceptance . . . Now, what do you do with it? How do you ground it into your behaviour, into your experience? How do you make it part of who you are?

And the first step, of course, is to love yourself. We harp on this—it is true—we go over and over it, but it is the only way. You are created in Love, by Love, for the purpose of expanding Love. By accepting that you have a mission, a purpose, a reason, for the breath that you breathe and the time that you are here, that you have a reason for being part of the great events that are occurring on the planet at this time and coming forward into Life, by accepting that you are the Beloved of The Divine and valued and valuable, exactly as you are, encouraged, supported indeed, to go beyond where you are . . .

But if you choose to stay exactly as you are now, there is no diminishment in that Love. We accept you completely, no matter what you do or do not do. You are part of our Love, and we are grateful for the opportunity of knowing each of you. Those who are your personal Guides and Guardians, very much, are delighted to have the opportunity and the experience of advancing their growth by being part of your lives.

When you participate in the Spirituality of Life at this point in time, you also understand that that spirituality is not separate from the rest of your life but is to be integrated into all that you do. By living your life from that perspective, that every choice you make, you can make to live in a positive way, in an uplifting way, in a healing way, in an encouraging way, for the benefit of the entire community of Life on the planet, then you are serving your highest purpose.

Now, there are times when you are tired. There are times when you are frustrated. There are times when you are just fed up with everybody else, and all you want to do is be selfish. Well go ahead; be centered in yourself; look after your needs; take the time; experience it; get it over with; get on with it—and then carry on and refocus, but for Heaven's sake, My Loves, do not harass and hound yourself because you were selfish for twenty minutes or 20 days. The fact of the matter is that you were looking after yourself. If you felt that you were being selfish and putting yourself first, it was because it was needed. You have such a concept about looking after yourselves that we would sometimes wish we could shake you out of it. "Yes," we have said to you, "If you do not look after yourselves and then you falter, or you fall, then how are you going to be of service to others," and so some of you say, "Okay, I'll take care of myself for the sake of others." Well, that's a start, but you need to take care of yourselves for your own sake, simply because it's you, simply because you are worthy of it.

If you are not worthy of this life and all the good that can come to you in this life, you wouldn't be here. You would never have been created. The Divine knows you're worthy. We know you're worthy. How is it that you don't know? Aren't you listening?

Wonderful Ones, you are listening but not to us. By accepting—at least at the beginning, that there might be the possibility that what we are saying here tonight is, indeed, that you are beautiful; you are worthy; you are precious to us beyond measure—by taking that as a theory, as a premise, that you might wish to contemplate or explore or investigate, and then trying it out by treating yourself as if you were that precious eminence, and treating yourself as if you were a valuable resource worthy of listening to your thoughts and your desires and your encouragement, that is a wonderful step to take. We would strongly encourage that, and if you feel that's being selfish, well, let us re-phrase it somewhat.

Let us take the concept of being self-centred and change it from its negative connotation to one that is saying, "I am centred, right here, in myself, and when I understand that I am centred in peace and in serenity and harmony, then I can move forward in such a way that I do not have to be out of balance with life," and so this is what we are encouraging you to do. This is what we are encouraging within you. Be self-centred. Focus on what you need in order for your life to be a blessed and pleasurable experience, then go and do it.

Each of you is a leader in your own way. As you follow your Life of Happiness and Joy, you are demonstrating to others how positive, how valuable, how delightful, that can be. You are saying to them, "Look, you've known me for twenty years. You know me. I'm no different from who you are. We both know that like attracts like. If I can do this, then you can do this. It's not rocket science. It's just making a choice. I choose to be happy," and by saying that, you give them permission to make that same choice—by understanding that your happiness resides in your choice to be happy and not in any circumstance or any other person.

Yes, having another person with you can expand your happiness, but your happiness does not have to reside in that other person. Your happiness resides in you. Your preference may be to have that other person as part of your life, and that is an excellent thing; but, by choosing to be happy anyway, you are free. You are not bound by any kind of change, to a circumstance, or an individual, because you know that life will change, and life often changes in an unexpected manner. If you have said, "I will be happy, with you with me," and something happens, and that individual is no longer in your life, are you ever going to be happy again?

How sad.

Because if that person has left the physical life, you know that they will want you to be happy, and if that person has gone on in their lives and is with another person, you know that they don't want you tied to them.

So it is important to accept that you are the Creator of your Life from the circumstances of how you are going to respond to Life's events, and as you decide that the sunshine of Joy is going to be what shines on you, is going to be the standpoint from which you make your decisions and your perceptions about Life, then you will find that Life is much lighter, that Life works a lot better, because you have made that decision. Ahhhh, My Loves, indeed—by accepting your power to create a life of Joy or a life of struggle, you are The Divinity in your Life.

You are the creative force in your life, and—I promise you—it is so much more fun to be happy. We strongly encourage each of you to take time every week—some of you we have said this to before, but we will repeat it again—it is well worth it—to take a two-hour period, two consecutive hours every week, where you do something that is creative and pleasurable.

It does not matter what. It is not about something being done perfectly, being done for anyone else, being done in any particular manner. It has two criteria: One, that it is creative; and two, that it is fun. After that, everything else is a bonus, and as you allow yourself this creativity-break every week, you will find that that creativity and that sense of fun flows into other areas of your life, without any kind of effort. It just moves there because it is an energy thing; because, like you, there are no boundaries on that type of energy. And so, it just sort of . . . smoothes its way, flows into the other parts of your life, and that is the purpose of this.

This is not to give you one more thing to do. You have lots. You may find that you want to give up something that isn't as much fun, and that would be a kind thing to do to yourselves, indeed.

Very much, we wish you Joy. Very much, we wish you laughter. It is the most effective and positive way of learning anything, especially any difficult thing—to let yourself laugh about it. Now, we understand that it is difficult for some of you to laugh at yourselves, but that's fine. Borrow a small child. Get yourself a small pet and laugh at them, and that will be the start of it.

You are so magnificent. As you accept yourselves as Our Beloved, then you will come to accept yourselves as your own Beloved, and at that point all of creation is yours.

Wonderful Ones, we are very grateful for the opportunity to have spent this time with you. We look forward to seeing you again, and be sure that we will see you. May the lovingness of God watch over your going out and your coming in. Take care of each other, and take care of yourselves.

We love you dearly. Be blessed in all that you do, and, above all, Dear Hearts—laugh.

## CHAPTER II

# Forgiveness

The Four Archangels gathered again with me to deliver their perspectives on "Forgiveness:" What—the Mind; Why—the Emotion; Where—the Practical; and When—the Spiritual Practice. The Archangels presenting were Gabriel, Raphael, Uriel, and Michael.

Understanding the importance and oftentimes the difficulty that surrounds the practice of Forgiveness, these loving Beings of Light want to stress the loving nature of Forgiveness. In particular, they want to emphasize that Forgiveness—by its very nature—is a gift to all parties concerned.

As always in this series, Archangel Gabriel began by sharing his view that Forgiveness is a Factor of the Mind or the Air Element which governs thoughts and communication, especially inner communication.

The Archangel Raphael addresses the Water or Emotional Element of Forgiveness when he speaks about the degree of intensity of various situations and how easy or difficult it can be to contemplate being forgiving.

Using the Fire or Inspiration Element, the Archangel Uriel encourages us to realize and accept the blessing nature of Forgiveness; that it can bring a richness and brightness into our lives.

From the Archangel Michael we are given the practical and spiritual means [Earth Element] of practising Forgiveness in our daily lives—as we have been encouraged to do in the praying and meditating ways of all the great religions and spiritual observations.

The Angels and I together hope you will discover the richness in the custom of mercy.

# A Factor of the Mind—Archangel Gabriel

Dear and Wonderful Ones, this is a great pleasure to talk on the subject that so many of you have such a struggle with, and we would hope in the course of your evening that we are able to change your orientation, to encourage you to understand what a delightful situation can arise when you move into the energy of Forgiveness.

First of all, I would like you to understand that Forgiveness is not for the other person. It has nothing to do with the other person except that it gives them the opportunity to be free, free of a situation that ties both of you karmically, that ties both of you energetically, that ties both of you negatively, to an ongoing situation, to a situation that can continue to erode and irritate, in particular in a spiritual manner.

Forgiveness—what is it and what is it not? As we have said, it is not about the other person. Forgiveness is about yourself. Forgiveness does not dissolve karma, but Forgiveness allows you to move into the energy of the State of Grace, and it is Grace that dissolves karma. It is Grace that moves you from where you are to where you can be, in a bright, beautiful, harmonious, and loving manner, and so Forgiveness is the open door that leads you into that state. We would encourage you to consider very, very clearly the benefits to be attained from engaging in the practice of Forgiveness.

Forgiveness is one of the greatest activities you can engage in, in order to present to the world, to channel to the world—if you will—to share with the world your Highest Purpose, the basic purpose for which every individual incarnates; the purpose for which every individual Soul was created, and that is the sharing, the propagation, the transmission, the radiance, of Love. And Forgiveness is how Love is extended, is expanded, does its work, on this plane and on many others.

I would encourage you to understand that Forgiveness is one energy that absolutely must come from a clear and willing Heart.

Forgiving, because it is the right thing to do even when you don't want to do it, isn't forgiving.

Forgiving, because you then move yourself into a better and brighter energy, will not work well.

Forgiving, because you "should", is ineffective. It is not true forgiving.

And Forgiving without forgetting, My Loves, is not forgiving at all. When you say to an individual, "Well, I'll forgive you, but I won't forget," that is not Forgiveness at all.

Very, very clearly, you can tell from the energy; often you can tell from the body language, with arms crossed and some degree of displeasure on the face, but I say to you that when you set out to forgive others, make it a three-sixty exercise, make it a w/holistic exercise, and forgive yourself as well.

There are those of you who will say, "Well, why do I have to forgive myself. They did it to me."

Sorry, doesn't work like that.

Forgiveness comes into necessity, or requirement, or the greatest gift—for it is a gift that you can give yourself and others—forgiveness comes into effect, when you and others use Free Will to take yourself onto the clearest path of generating and radiating Love energy. It is a construct of the behaviour of this world, of this Life.

Forgiveness eases your path. Forgiveness releases tension and stress, and all of you have more than enough stress in your lives, at this point in time, you really don't need another big helping.

So, when you can say:

> I'm tired of carrying this burden. I don't have a strong, positive resonance for that person, and because of that, because of my anger, because of my frustration, because of the negativity between us, because I want to blame this other person rather than taking responsibility myself, I am tied to that person, and whether I never see them again in this Lifetime there is still that tie.

There is still that issue and that energy that needs to be worked out, that needs to be balanced, that ties you again to a cycle of another Lifetime here. So what will you do? You're the one with Free Will. Yes—it's true—they have Free Will as well, but they may not even be affected by the situation that has you in an outrage.

It's your issue; it's your feelings; it's your perception; therefore, it's your responsibility.

A very wise individual once said—and this quotation has, the ability to cause a great deal of upset, but know, Dear Hearts, that this applies to each and every one of you. So, if you become upset, forgive me for creating the condition, or the circumstance, or the environment, where you can choose to be upset, but forgive yourselves for being upset—

The quotation is:

> If there's a problem, I caused it, either by my action or by my reaction, and even if the problem did not originate with me, I must take responsibility for its solution, in order to bring us to peace.

And so, this is not about blame. Forgiveness is not interested in blame; Forgiveness is interested in harmony. It is a gift you give into the world; it is a gift you give to yourself.

Forgiveness is, as the word says; it is for-giving.

It gives you the opportunity to go beyond the energy state that you are in, to transcendent it, to bring it to a greater sense of peace, to bring it to balance, to bring Joy back into your Life; because, when you are sitting in a non-forgiving state, when you are sitting in anger, and frustration, and blame, and finger-pointing, and fault finding, you cannot be harmonious. You cannot be serene. You are not in a State of Love. Forgiveness leads the way to a greater degree of Love.

If you say, "I can love the whole world except that person," I say to you that that negative energy between you and that person permeates—crawls into—all your other relationships and erodes them, brings you to a state of imbalance in all your situations.

How difficult is it to say:

> I was a co-creator in this situation, and even if I can't face that about myself, this situation is disruptive, disharmonious, doesn't feel good for me, makes me think in a negative way about that person; therefore, it incites an energy within me that I don't like. It just isn't enough fun to carry on.

When you get to that stage, when you understand that this hard energy within you is cluttering up your radiance, then you can say to yourself, "I will forgive myself for being in this situation, and I will forgive this other individual for being in this situation as well."

Or you say:

> But, it's far too huge. The situation that has hurt me has knocked me so far off balance that I really am tempted to be bitter for the next sixteen

Lifetimes[1]. It was huge. I can't just say, "I forgive," and truly mean it, and have it over and done with.

And, that is an acceptable thing, for the moment that you are in, but understand that all Life is Change, and Forgiveness sets up a more powerful and more dynamic change than you can imagine when you sit in your frustration.

Perhaps it is enormous in your Life. Perhaps you don't want to forgive them. Set it aside, but know that that energy is working, working, working, and it is working on you. So set it aside for the time being. Prepare yourself to know that you are going to come to a changed state, to understand that you are not going to stay in this unrelenting energy, provided you are willing to work the other energies in your Life.

In other areas of your Life, if you choose to be loving, that Loving vibration wants to go over to this area where you have set no Forgiveness. If you are considerate about other people; if other people are compassionate and considerate toward you, those energies want to go over to this holding space and clear that up as well, and one day the Light will go on; one day Life will be worth living everywhere, except there, and then you are brought back to the situation again, but because you have shifted your energy, you are going to be brought back to a situation where—now you have to deal with it.

Either you are going to have to deal with this issue of, "Will I or won't I forgive this person," or "Am I going to risk contamination? Do I want to be involved with this person for the next sixteen, bitter Lifetimes?"

Because every Lifetime that you are involved with that vibration, with that situation, with that individual, the price goes up. It gets tougher every time.

For those of you who love logic, we would say, is it not more logical to forgive at the outset or as close to that as you can, rather than having to go through this again? You thought you were clobbered this time. Just wait 'till you get to Round Sixteen, because, by then, that person will have had the chance to hit you back.

So give yourself the gift. Give all others with whom you come into contact, that gift. Give that person the gift, if only at first, so that you are not tied to them again.

Now, that is a form of . . . desiring to control your outcomes, but if that is the only step that you can take at the beginning, then take it. If

---

[1] See Questions and Answers, Page 211, Archangel Michael's response to "Sixteen Lifetimes"

THE FOUR ARCHANGELS

the only step that you can take at the beginning is to say, "God, I cannot forgive this person. Will you forgive them for me?" and God will say, "I will do it provided . . . provided you continue to release yourself and work on Forgiveness from your heart to theirs. I will not do it for you, but I will do it as a prelude to your doing your own forgiving."

It does not affect God, one way or the other, if you choose not to forgive this person, but it does affect you, and it affects all who come into your vibration.

How can you expect—with the individuals in this world becoming more and more intuitive, more and more sensitive, more and more telepathic—how can you expect them to perceive your energy as clear, pure, healing, and loving if there is this underlying rot of unwillingness to forgive, because it permeates your vibration?

It gives a sense of falseness to all these positive qualities you would share with others. Forgiveness is the way to releasing yourself from this ball-and-chain, and as I have said very often, it is you who is affected. The other person is going merrily on their way, may not even be aware of the intensity of the hurt that you have been feeling, because that's in your Universe. That's in the way you perceive, but that is not necessarily in the way that this other person perceives Life.

We will remind you of the sayings: "As within, so without. What goes around, comes around." All of these start with you. You are the Point of Origin. You are the source of your experiences and your expression in Life. The trials and tribulations that you undergo are on your Life agenda, put there in your own hand, accepted by you with the agreement of the Most High and your Council of Twelve[2], and in the case of interaction with other people, in agreement with them and their Councils of Twelve as well. You agreed to it. You agreed to try this out, to see what you could do to move beyond the human attitude and to forgive and to love no matter what.

James the Apostle, said over and over and over, "Little children, love one another," and that includes forgiving them, because Forgiveness does not come from Love—forgiveness comes from hate—if it is withheld.

When it is given freely with no strings attached, it is the entry to Unconditional Love. It is the way-shower, the door-opener, for Divine Love.

Dear Hearts, it is one of the most difficult things that you can do in your Life. It is also one of the most healing things that you can do in your Life.

---

[2] See Questions and Answers, Page 211, for Archangel Michael's answer on the Council of Twelve

Forgiving is the gift that you give the World. Yes, your focus might be on this one individual, but their Life has changed, and your Life has changed, and like two stones dropped into a puddle, the rings that intermix, the rings that hit each other, are points where other people who have connected to you and connected to this other person are touched as well. And so that Radiance of Forgiveness goes outward. It clears your vibration. It solidifies your sincerity.

It makes itself known to others that you are a compassionate healer who can forgive, which means that they can go to you with their trauma, with their self-judgment, with their uncertainty, and say, "Here is who I am, warts and all. Can you love me anyway?"

If your intention, and if your practice, is to be of a clear, loving vibration, forgiving everything, then you can say, "Yes, I love you," and they will know that it is true, and they will know that you are bringing forth Divine, Healing Love. But if there is this cyst festering in your background, there is no healing there, not even for you.

We encourage you to ask your Guides and Guardians to help you;

To ask the Most High;

To ask those Angels and Archangels that have the greatest resonance for you;

To ask the Ascended Masters;

To ask All Bright Spirits everywhere to assist you in coming to this State of Forgiveness, for your sake as well as the other person's sake.

There are some of you who have heard of the protocol, we shall say, for writing to the Guardian Angels, and I would include that procedure here:

Every night or every day, whenever it is convenient, for 15 nights—this is the ancient number of completion—so it will bring the situation to completion for you. It is also the vibration of beauty, and so it will bring a beautiful situation into you. This is moving from outside, non-beneficial influence to the decision for Love. That is what the 15 to the six is.

Now, you write a brief note to the Guardian Angel of this person, and your own Guardian Angel. The two of you are in this situation. The two of you obviously need work, and in that letter, brief note—it does not have to go on for pages—but in that brief note you say:

> 'Help us release the disruptive, negative energy between us. Please give us the wisdom and the love to make good decisions for ourselves to benefit both of us and to bring healing and harmony to our situation . . .' and whatever else your intuition and your compassion would encourage you to write.

At the end of the 15 nights you burn all the letters. In this regard those energies at that point are released very dynamically.

There are two provisions: *Firstly*, because this is a highly sensitive instrument, you say nothing, in particular to the person that you are writing on behalf of. You say nothing to anyone else of what you are doing. It takes very little of a disbelieving attitude to diminish the energy of this to work for you, and *[Secondly,]* if you see progress before the end of the 15th night, it is important to complete all of those nights; otherwise, the energy dissipates, and all the progress that you have made is lost.

We have reminded you before that your Guides and Guardians, your Angels, stand waiting to be asked to assist in your Life, to offer their guidance, to offer their encouragement, to offer their support, their healing, but you must ask.

If it feels to you that it is a lack of independence, that it is a weakness for you, to ask, disabuse yourself of that idea. The asking requirement is in place because you have Free Will, and we will never force upon you that which you have not chosen.

When you choose Forgiveness, you are stepping up to a higher vibration. You are stepping onto the path that leads to serenity, that ensures that when you need Forgiveness, it is there waiting for you, because as you give to another so are you given, as you withhold for another so it is withheld from you. The Law is very balanced in that regard and I say to you as well there is no one here who continues in Life who does not need forgiving. So long as you are present on the Earth plane, there is a potential that you could use a good helping of Forgiveness. If you give it to yourself, it is much more palatable than if you wait, holding your breath and begging, for someone else to give it to you, and as you would wish to be treated, with generosity, with healing and with compassion, so too we would encourage you to treat others in this manner.

Dear and Wonderful Ones, giving yourself the gift of Forgiveness, when you forgive another, is indeed a way of communicating To All Life Everywhere that you are a healer, that your steps are on the path toward The Divine, and that you are doing very well indeed, and the circumstances of your Life shift to reflect that. May you know the Joy of releasing yourself and the Other from the lines of energy that imprison you.

Be blessed in all that you do.

# A Feeling of the Heart—Archangel Raphael

Dear Hearts, I wish to address *the why* of Forgiveness. We have said some things about why you could forgive; why it is a good idea to forgive; why it is a blessing to forgive; but, I wish to address the feelings of it.

When a situation first arises, when you hold it in stasis and do not allow the energy to change; when you keep it stable, the way that it was when it first hit you, your tendency is to say, "Why should I?"

Now, the first thing that I would like to do is address the word "should." This is a judgment. It is not an evaluation. This is a form of dictating to yourself or another, what you deem appropriate or right. It has nothing to do with justice. It has nothing to do with fairness. It is always a judgment against, and therefore we strongly recommend that when you use this word that it becomes hot, that it flashes, that it becomes very loud, so that your awareness of the use of this word becomes much more intense.

We wish you, as well, to understand that *should* elevates one person over another, and when you use it against yourself, by saying, "I should have, or I should . . . whatever," you are holding yourself in a state of wrongness. You are holding yourself in a state of being criticized, undeserving, and unworthy, and it is an unjust position to put yourself in.

There is no true Forgiveness if the word *should* is involved, and so if you are saying to yourself, "Well, I want to be more spiritual. I want to be more loving. I want to be more like the God of My Understanding; therefore, I *should* forgive," you are not doing it for the right reasons.

You are setting yourself up to be dictated to. You are setting yourself up to be wrong once more, for you do judge yourself over and over, so tremendously.

Dear Hearts, when you relax the energy, when you say to yourself:

This state of non-Forgiveness is a drain on my energy, disturbs my digestion, interferes with my sleep. It is not a beneficial energy for me; therefore, I will consider my options:

(1) I could forgive them.
(2) I could hold on to it.
(3) I could ask for help.
(4) I could see a psychologist.
(5) I could pray to my angels.
(6) I could turn my back on the whole situation, bury it deep within me, and never allow myself to think of it again.

So I have many options. Now, what I need to discover is what is going to be the best for both of us?

This is a situation that is not for you alone. There is yourself and the Other, but the question is, "How do you feel about forgiving this person?" Perhaps someone took a swipe at your vehicle and damaged it, and now you have all of this hassle, and hoo-rah, and difficulty, to go through, and it is such a pain in the neck, and in the pocketbook, and uses up your time. Why would you want to forgive that person?

Because, a hundred years from now, is that going to be of consequence?

A year from now, is that going to be of consequence?

That may be the tack that you could take. In the grand scheme of things this is of less consequence. It is of less importance, but what if, in the hitting of your vehicle, a Life was lost.

Now that state of woundedness has been elevated a great deal more. Now what are you going to do? How do you feel about this?

Yes, you want to blame this other person.

Yes, you want to point fingers.

Yes, you want them to experience justice according to your definition of justice.

What are you going to do? Can you forgive? Are you able to? That, at first, is just as equal a question to consider as, are you *willing* to forgive the person?

Are you able to?

Perhaps you want to so that you can be released from the intense negativity of the situation, from the reminders over and over and over; for your own sake, so that you don't have to be involved with stress leave from work, or medications from your physician, or things of this nature, to absolve yourself of the nightmares of running over this situation again and again, and then you look at it, "Can I do this?"

And immediately within you, up jumps this outraged little feeling that says, "No, that person has to pay. I was hurt. They did it. They have to pay," but I say to you, Dear Hearts—and be very clear on this—you cannot have a situation in your Life—from the stubbing of a toe to the breaking of a fingernail, to the breaking of a heart, to the loss of a Life—you can have no situation in your Life that you didn't agree to before you came in. Everything is an opportunity for your growth, and your healing, and your advancement, in spirituality and sharing love. Every single circumstance is an opportunity.

What are you going to do with it? What are you going to do about it? This person, you feel, has wounded you. Do you understand the circumstances that this person has gone through? Perhaps you have had a difficulty in your past, forgiving other situations, getting past them, and you hold yourself stuck, and wounded, and tormented, lifetime after lifetime after lifetime and this person comes into your Life to create a tremendous situation to give you that opportunity to say:

> No more, no more hurt, no more pain, no more difficulty, no more intensity! I forgive. I forgive God. I forgive this other person. I forgive me. I forgive the whole world, because I choose to move out of pain. I choose a Life of healing, not victimization. I choose to find the sunlight sparkling, not dreary days. I choose to move into Life.

Why do these things happen? Very often, it is difficult, from the human perspective, to understand why these things happen, and the more intense; the more difficult it is to know. When the planes dove into the twin towers in September, years past, what occurred there was an agreement. It was tragic, yes; but I say to you that the American peoples and the Peoples of the Earth had refused to listen, over and over and over, until all that was left was an impact, to understand what was being done around the world, to understand the imbalances that had been occurring, to bring attention to situations of imbalance, to bring attention to situations that need forgiving, and yet how many people will say, "I will never forgive that event,"—on both sides.

The reluctance to forgive, to be compassionate, to say, "I'm standing here in the mud with you," not, "I'm standing up here at the top of the hole tossing down a rope, and if you catch it, fine, and if you don't, too bad," to say, "I share your burden. I share your pain, and I will therefore share in healing your situation."

That is why that situation arose, because both parties felt justified in holding their points of view and were unwilling to hear, or forgive, or be compassionate, toward the other point of view.

Could that situation have been avoided? Yes.

Will that situation occur again? Possibly.

It all depends on how the Peoples of the Earth are willing to work with their feelings and to move away from destructiveness towards healing, towards Love, toward overriding and dissolving and diminishing those situations that appear to be unforgivable.

Why would you want to forgive? We have focused on it as beneficial for you. What about this other person? This person who has done something that you judge to be an attack on yourself, to be harmful to yourself, to be negative toward yourself.

Why would you want to forgive them? And we will say that the Forgiveness is for Peace on Earth. The Forgiveness is for your spiritual evolvement. The Forgiveness happens so Life can become worthwhile once again, and you can smile, and you can laugh, and you can heal, and you can enjoy Life, and you can make others understand that there is a purpose to this.

You may not understand why this had to happen. There is a saying that until you get to the point that you don't need to know why, you will never know why.

Suffice to say that circumstances happen because individuals make choices that lead to those circumstances. Some of them are on your agenda to be dealt with in a clear and open manner, for your self-growth, to give you the opportunity to say:

> This is what it feels like, but I choose not to stay in that energy. I choose to go beyond this. I will not propagate in the world any more negativity than is already here, and the only way that I can get past that, the only way I can dissolve that, the only way I can heal that, the only way I can take care of it so it won't come back and bite me in the back, is to forgive it.

When you have a situation where you choose not to forgive, what is occurring in the physical body is that, essentially, you are stepping on the hose, or the vein, or the transmission, of positive energy in your physical body, and that causes a build up, and it becomes bigger, and bigger, and bigger, until your heart explodes, because you could not release that pain, and no one wants your heart to explode.

If you try to deny something, to bury it, to lock it in a trunk in the back of your mind and put straps on it, and pile other stuff on it, and hide it away and forget it, as if it never happened—we will never talk of this again. It never happened—for a long time, it may appear that that's a good solution, but that energy has not been dissolved, that situation has not been resolved. It just sits there and festers and rots its way through that trunk, and then it boils up within you, and all the contamination of not forgiving spreads through your system.

There is a saying: This person is a thorn in my side.

Let me say to you that a thorn in your side leads to blood poisoning and blood is the energy of Life. It is the physical representation of Life Force energy. So, if a person is a thorn in your side, they are poisoning you, until *you* pull that thorn out and deal with it.

How much pain do you want to be in?

You have Free Will. It's your choice. If you cannot forgive in order to be a blessing to the other person, which is the highest emanation of this situation, then forgive so that you can heal yourself, and you will come to know that after you are healed because you have forgiven; then the next stage is, indeed, to forgive that other person, to absolve them, to say to them:

> I know you had a lesson for me. It wasn't a great lesson. It was very difficult, but I survived. I am stronger because you were in my Life. I still don't like you, and that is not a requirement of Forgiveness.

Louise Hay has given one of the most powerful and generous recommendations for forgiving an individual, yourself, a circumstance, and she says:

> Say to the situation; say to the other person—whether physically, in each other's presence, by writing it, by meditating and connecting with this person—say to them, 'I forgive you for not being the person I wanted you to be, and I forgive myself for being in this situation with you. I forgive us both, and I set us both free.'[3]

Imagine . . . being free . . . how wonderful, how uplifting, how exciting, how healing, how loving. Each of you, when you enter into circumstances with people—whether it is a relationship, whether it is a happenstance, whether it is a collision—when that occurs, you have an expectation, and sometimes people don't meet your expectations.

Well, guess what? Sometimes you don't meet their expectations either.

It's okay, so long as you do not get so emotionally overwrought about their being wrong, their being not the way you wanted, that you interfere with the potential of transcending that, with the potential of going

---

[3] "You Can Heal Your Life". Louise L. Hay, Hay House Publishing Inc., 1984

beyond your expectation and to discovering, in that person, someone very worthwhile. Can you take Forgiveness to that degree?

It is an amazing thing if you can, but the requirement is to be of a very forgiving nature. Forgiveness always brings forth Love. Gabriel has said this. The Christ has said this. On the cross He said, "Father, forgive them. They know not what they do," and when you forgive another, can you forgive them from that loving standpoint, knowing that in many circumstances you have had the opportunity for a greater knowledge, a greater awareness, a greater understanding, of the trueness of Life than most people that you will meet, certainly those people that you meet on a casual basis, and can you, therefore, move into that vibration of the Christ and say, "I forgive you. I know you didn't know what you were doing. I forgive you, and I set us both free?" No karma, no cords, no requirement to come back with this individual or with a similar vibration and take the test again, and then after you have forgiven them, love yourself.

Love yourself for having passed another test, not in an egotistical way but in a way that says, "Love is why I'm here. I have done well. It may have been difficult, but I have done very well. I am pleased," and your Guides and Guardians will say: "As are we, let us love you more." Forgive for your sake. Forgive for the sake of The Divine. Forgive as you follow the example of the Christ. Forgive even for the other person's sake. Forgive for the Planet's sake, so that peace has a greater chance, but, above all, forgive, at first, because you don't want to, and then because you do want to.

We love you greatly. You are a Joy to us, and we know, with your great, good intentions, you will continue to be so.

# The Inspiring Spirit—Archangel Uriel

Dear and Wonderful, Glorious Beings of Light, how can we inspire you with Forgiveness?

It has, for many of you, such a connotation of hard, hard work, but I say to you, it is the uplifting step to that which brings Life back to a meaningfulness, to a delight, to a passion. It allows you to open up at a much more dynamic vibration, a much more enthusiastic way of being in the world. When you are holding the energy of non-Forgiveness, what is happening is that it siphons off all your Joy in Life, and that is what it does.

Forgiveness blesses you. It blesses all in the world. It allows the energy of "ahhhhh"—serenity, compassion, soothingness—to come back into your Life, but this is not an energy that you can hold for yourself. As you continue, as Life moves forward, as you fill yourself with the release, and the satisfaction, and the completeness of having forgiven, it pounds from you; it dances from you; it touches other people, and they know that you have become a sanctuary of safety, that you have become a person who can hear difficulty and bear it in such a way that you can uplift not only yourself but themselves as well.

It allows you to move into another of the purposes for which you came, which is to bring healing energy. Love is healing energy. Healing encourages everyone, as our friend Raphael says, "[Healing] Encourages everyone to Attain Love." That is what healing is for.

Any situation where you withhold Forgiveness, you are withholding healing from yourself and others. Not just the person that is involved in this situation with you, but any other person that you would touch in a positive way.

Let us encourage you. When you decide that you want a more loving vibration, when you look at the circumstances in your Life, and you understand that there are certain blocks, that things are not flowing in the positive way that you would have them, it is important for you to take a look . . . "Where do I need to put more love? If there is not more love there, why has that not occurred." Chances are it was because there is a need for a greater degree of release, of compassion, which we would say is Forgiveness. By releasing this person from connection to you and doing it in the most loving manner, you give them the opportunity to go beyond where they are. You give them another chance to find a positive solution.

We find individuals who go through the process of ending relationships, whether it is simply an "I-don't-want-to-be-in-relationship-with-you-any-longer," or it involves the greater unwinding, unravelling, of divorce, or whatever. When the next relationship comes along for you, and you are finding that things are not going well, even though you've done work with an image, even though you have understood very clearly what you need in a relationship, what you desire to have in a relationship, and you have worked on that with your Guides and Guardians, and yet there seems to be something not quite right; something blocks it; something holds it off.

Maybe the relationship that you have worked so hard for doesn't even manifest, and that is when you need to go back over the previous relationship that you have had, and say to it, and say to yourself, "What have I left unfinished? What does this old relationship need from me in order that it can be at peace, and I can then move forward?"

This is what needs to happen. This is what needs to be taken a look at. In any circumstance . . . if you find that your finances are clogged, and clogged, and clogged—your finances are a representation of how you value yourself, how worthy you feel you are, how wonderful you feel you are. If you have left a situation where there is not at least a neutral feeling about that other individual, there is something that is standing in the way of your creating that positive evaluation of yourself, and when you look at that, you will know what it is you need to forgive in yourself, and perhaps in the Other as well, that will then allow you to step into a radiant, flowing stream of Life's energy. As our friend Abraham calls it, "Being in the Stream is when Life simply flows, and it happens joyously, joyfully, with great ease."

If that is not where you are, then what is recommended is that you say to your Life, "Okay Life, I'm sitting right here. I want you to tell me—what is this about? Where do I still need to do some work? Where do I still need to release and free myself from circumstances that are interfering"—and when that occurs, then you will find that you are beginning to live a conscious Life, an inspired Life.

That is what you are here for: to live a Life that allows you to experience great, good Joy; to live a Life that allows you to know what Abundance is; to know what Friendships are at the deepest, most encouraging level; to have a Life work that fills you with happiness, with a feeling of purpose, with a feeling of doing something that you can be proud of and that others can take pleasure in. When your Life works at the very highest flow, then Love is what is directing you. It is as if Love stands at the guiding point of your gondola and serenades you with beauty, as you continue on your journey.

If you are running the rapids one more time, then another layer needs to be dealt with. There are some people that you can forgive . . . and just—over and done with—one layer. There are other circumstances where it takes layer, after layer, after layer, and the first layer is for the other person, and the second layer may be for the fact that this circumstance occurred to you at all; and so that second layer is for The Divine, for you to come to a point of Trust in The Divine again; of knowing that that Great Being always has your Highest Good in Its Mind, in Its Desire for you, and the other layers are for yourself and your growth.

It may be easy to forgive a person on an intellectual level but that's not the only level. That is Mind. It will be more difficult, with difficult circumstances, to forgive individuals on a Heart level, an emotional level, and you may have to forgive yourself, and open yourself to the Love that you can give yourself, in order to process, in order to work with that positive vibration for you, and then there is the spiritual part of it.

The spiritual part of it can often be the easiest because all it needs from you is to bring in that Soul Consciousness, that part of you that wants all of Life to be nothing but an expression of Love, and when you bring that in, when you allow that energy through, the spiritual part is solved as well.

And what about the practical?

What about the child, abused when very young, who, because of that abuse, manifests the challenge of Cerebral Palsy, for example? Every single day they have an awareness that someone created a condition that has caused them this circumstance, this body that does not quite work the way it could, the way it was intended, the way it was born to be, and yet I say to you that even there, there is an opportunity for you to say, "I was in agreement with this circumstance so that I could become more of a Divinely Encouraged, Loved, and Radiant Being. So now that I've got this, what am I going to do with it?"

Those of you who have experienced the intensity of migraine headaches will understand that with migraines comes a choice—and if you get them frequently, this choice is very clear—either you go to bed for the rest of your Life as an invalid, or you work around it, and when you choose to work around that Pillar of Pain, you become very strong, but more importantly you become very inspirational. And so, you forgive yourself for allowing this circumstance into your Life. You say, "Okay, I picked it. I had an agreement with it. This happened to me for a reason. What's the best I can make of it? Where can I take this?"

With an individual who is torn from your Life, what are you going to do? Are you going to solidify yourself, stabilize yourself, hold yourself in that static energy of unforgiving dislike, despair, depression, hatred for All Life Everywhere, or are you going to say, "This is what has occurred. I cannot change it. I can only change me. If I want to go through this again, I will stay here in this energy, and I will never forgive,"

But, I promise you, Wonderful Ones that any situation that is static and relentlessly stable becomes distorted, becomes so stuck that there is no growth. There is no progress, good, bad, or indifferent. There is only dissolution. There is only rotting. There is only dissolving. That which does not change to grow, dies; and even though the essence of Forgiveness is mental and emotional; nonetheless, it has a way of dealing, of out-picturing, in the way that you are inspired or despaired, in the way that you hold yourself in depression and begin to diminish your Life or in the way that you take your cue from others who have been in similar circumstances and let their inspiration inspire you because then you become the focal point, and your ability to transcend these difficult circumstances inspires others.

This is the point of the Wounded Healer. This is the point where you work on that situation which has the greatest difficulty for you, in order to heal the situation, and whether you succeed or not is immaterial. What is occurring here is the effort, the willingness to say, "I will not stay bound and held here, but I will take the little steps that I can to progress," and others around you will say:

> Look at this person. Look at the difficulties that they've gone through, and yet they can smile, and yet they can move into a vibration that allows them peace, that they are not filled with hatred, that they are filled with the intention and the clarity to have a Life of serenity, a Life of beauty.

It is your choice. Will you be hard-hearted and hold fast to this difficult situation, knowing that the tension of holding fast to it spreads itself through your body and adds great tension to all the circumstances of your Life, or will you allow yourself the gift of peace? The greatest saying that has ever been created amongst the Peoples of the Earth has come from the Essenes. They used to say, "Peace be with you." "Pax vobiscum," as the Romans learnt to say it.

From that vibration all else is built. When you are in peace, you are open to love. When you are in peace, you are open to receive all the bounty, all the benefits, all the beauty, of Life.

When you say to any other individual, "Peace be with you," you are saying to the planet, "Peace be with you," and when there is peace on a planetary scale, then all Life breaths, and expands, and becomes much more delightful, growth-oriented, harmonious.

All Life Everywhere becomes a sanctuary. When you say to the Earth in your meditations, "Peace be with you," at the deepest level there is planetary healing. At the highest level there is another degree, another molecule, another breath, into ascension, but if you are not filled with peace in your heart, then you need peace to be with you.

Understand that when you say anything to anyone, you are saying it to yourself as well. So, (laughing) "Watch your mouth!"

When you say to someone, "Peace be with you," it resonates within you.

When you say to someone, "I will not forgive you," it resonates within you.

When you say to someone, "I love you," it resonates within you.

When you say, "I forgive you," it resonates within you.

Very much, what you say—and for individuals such as yourselves, working on expanding your Mastery, what you think, also—has a great deal of influence. Now, you know that your thoughts are the originating point. That is where things are created. That is where circumstances are created, but there are people who say, "I only thought it. I didn't say it."

Well, in your case, My Loves, you don't have that out, not anymore. So, you need to watch your thoughts, and weed out those thoughts that do not bring you Joy, that do not bloom with possibility and potential, and beauty, and delight, within you.

When you say, "Peace be with you," and you understand that you are saying—to The Source within you, to your Essence, to your Soul—you are saying, "Peace be with you," deep within yourself. That sets forth the vibration that is irresistible to such energies as I-will-not-forgive. The two cannot coexist, but Peace has the power. And so, when you say, "Peace be with you," you are saying it to yourself, and you are empowering yourself to go beyond the situation that is holding you captive.

If your state of mind is such anguish that you cannot say to another person or another circumstance, "I am ready to forgive you," then say to yourself, "Peace be with you," and that readiness to forgive will be given one more deposit, one more piece of empowering energy, so that you can get there. We do not expect that you will instantaneously convert to the religion of Forgiveness. All we ask of you is that you do not stay in the darkness where you have been, for some of you in the darkness where you are.

All we are saying is: make the intention, and every day reaffirm that intention. Make the saying "Peace be with you," make the saying "I love you," make the saying "I am willing to move toward Forgiveness."

All that we are asking for, all that we are encouraging you to do, all that we are loving and supporting you to do, is to take the first step. Entertain the possibility that at some point you may be at a willingness to forgive. That allows you to take one step towards that, and then, all you need is one more step, but the first is most difficult, and once you have taken that first one, it is infinitely easier to take that second one, and every step you take toward that serenity, that letting go, that release, that self-empowerment, is one step more toward the experience of The Divine Love that is within you.

Forgiveness involves the words *for-giving*. It is a gift you give yourself. It is a gift you give your planet. It is a gift you give your God, and then, somewhere down the road, it is a gift you give the person that has wounded you, but first it goes to yourself because you are the most worthy. It is your Universe after all.

Do you wish to have enjoyment in your Universe?

Do you wish to have serenity and sacredness in your Universe?

Then, treat yourself to all of those qualities. Treat yourself to that degree of Love. At any moment, your Angels, your Guides and Guardians, and we, are available to assist you. Sometimes, those who Guide and Guard you stand wringing their hands around you, waiting for you to, "Please ask." They are never apart from you. They are always with you. It does not have to be elaborate. It does not have to be ceremonial—a thought that says, "Oh help."—They're there. The help is there.

When you love yourself more, Life begins to be more sparkling. You can laugh more. Some of you could use a little practice with that; and so, we will encourage it, but, whatever your choice, you cannot diminish Our Love for you by one iota. We love you wholly, exactly as you are. We love you magnificently. We love you far more than this whole planet could contain. Let us love you more, indeed.

# The Practical Practise—Archangel Michael

Dearly Beloved, and so, we get to the practical situation with Forgiveness. How do you forgive?

And, of course, it needs to be an evolution. Forgiving comes after you centre yourself, after you get past the intensity of the situation. Forgiveness is not an instantaneous thing. It is part of the grieving process, but it comes at the end, and every circumstance where Forgiveness comes into play is a circumstance where you are grieving a situation that could have been or a situation that was and that has shifted and changed.

So how do you get there? Indeed, the first thing that we would recommend that you do is to take a gentle time with yourself, none of this "shoulding," none of this, "Well, it's been x amount of time . . ." Just allow yourself to be patient with yourself. Work with yourself on a daily basis. Remind yourself that you are a child of The Divine.

We have made this recommendation in other circumstances, but it is such an important and an excellent tool:

> We will suggest that you get yourself sheets of scrap paper and different coloured markers, and that you get yourself a journal that you love and that you wish to use for your support and your positive encouragement.
>
> Take the papers, take markers that represent the colours of your feelings—if you are angry, and anger is red and black to you, use those—and begin to put your feelings down. If you like words, put your feelings down in words. If you like the movement of colour put it down like that. If you want to use paint, if you want to get your hands in and get real messy, go for it. Get the feelings out. Let yourself feel the intensity, the depth, the power, of those feelings, and put it all down on the paper.
>
> If you write so fast that the paper tears, keep writing. This is not about going back over this.
>
> This is an energy exercise to move that out of whom you are, onto the paper. The paper is like the receptacle, for this energy that needs to be released, and having done that, keep going, keep going, keep going until you are tired, until you feel empty. Let yourself quickly scan the body. Is there any place where you are holding that hard, tight, angry energy? Scoot it out of there. Suck it out of that place, and put it on the paper, and then take a breath.

Wrap those papers all up, and remove them from your environment. This is not about keeping it overnight for the garbage collection or next week until you get around it. This is getting this energy mass out of your environment; so it is gone, and then you come back in, and now you start the healing process.

Now you start to be gentle with yourself. You might have a cup of tea, a beverage that you find soothing. You might have a bit of a snack that allows you to start the process of rebuilding your energy.

You sit with this book that is so attractive, with a writing instrument that you find easy and fun to use, and begin there to write down positive things, to write down the number of blessings equivalent to your age, and I say to you that that is not a great many.

Blessings do not have to be miraculous. They do not have to be tricky. Allowing yourself the blessing of a cool, soothing place to sleep—that is a blessing. Having heard the song of your favourite bird, or the sight of your favourite bird—that is a blessing. So, you write down all those blessings, and then you write down how good it feels to be free of the chains that have bound you, and you are focusing on that freedom, and you are focusing on that good feeling.

You are not entertaining how it did feel when you were not in a positive state, and when you have done that, celebrate.

Do something for yourself that allows you to feel nurtured, nourished, cared for, cared about, loved, supported, congratulated because you have just done a mighty piece of work. You might consider having a hot stone massage, a luxurious thing, indeed. You might find that you wish to go in and have a bath with bubbles up to your chin, with aromatherapy moving through the room, and soothing your feelings with candles, with music that is relaxing and comforting. Perhaps you would have with you, your favourite book. That also encourages you, just to let you know how great a work you have done, and how much to be congratulated you are for this achievement, for this accomplishment.

You might feel like going out and celebrating, going to karaoke, going dancing, whatever it is that let's you feel congratulations for the work that you have done, for the fine, loving, healing work that you have done. It is important that you continue with this positive vibration; and therefore, we would recommend that as part of your on-going loving and cherishing of yourself for the work of release and Forgiveness, that every day you put in three more positive things that have occurred during the course of that day. When you do these things, then—coming on to a situation where your tendency is to move into, "I-will-never-forgive-you," modality again—you can go to your book.

When you find despair arises, when you find disruption occurs, you can go to your book, and see how wonderful your Life is.

We would suggest that the day before the Full Moon or, more particularly, the New Moon, the day before these occur, that you take some time, and say to yourself:

> This is the time when I am ready to clear my energy. I may choose to use sage and sweet-grass. I may choose to use an aromatherapy that is called Unconditional Love. I may choose to use the balancing of crystals around myself, or meditation, or just the fulfillment within myself of the knowledge and awareness that I have very much nurtured and cared for myself over this last moon cycle.

And having done that, on the New Moon you are then prepared to create in your Life, to bring forward in your Life, those circumstances that have the greatest value to you. And so, you write down a creation list—every New Moon or within forty eight hours of the New Moon, within eight hours if possible, but for Heaven's sake, if the New Moon occurs at midnight, and you don't get up until 9:30, don't wake yourself at four o'clock in the morning; don't stay up late unless you usually do. You still have the time—and you write down a minimum of two to a maximum of ten things that you desire in an easy and graceful way, in a healthy and positive way, to see come into your Life.

And, if you have done this cleansing of yourself at the Full Moon, then to go through the same procedure after the point of the Full Moon and release from your Life, with ease and grace, with serenity, with delight, those circumstances that you no longer wish or have a need for in your Life. By working on this on an ongoing basis, to keep your energy clear, to focus on that which you love—watching that—know that the Universe will interpret whatever you pay the most attention to as that which you Love.

So I'm saying to you, all of those with a dominant Virgo energy, if you love to worry, and you focus on your worries, the Universe will allow that to expand, because obviously you love worrying—"as you wish."

So by focusing on the positive in your Life, by focusing on the reasons why Life is worthwhile, you are keeping your energy strong and clear, and you have less and less reason to go through the ritual of Forgiveness, because you are not creating situations that require this of you. When you are seeking to come from the state of disruption to the state of serenity, so that you can deal with Life in a forgiving manner—as we have mentioned this is a grieving process.

You are allowed to be angry, angry at whomever you see as the participant in an unhealthy or unhappy situation in your Life. If you want to blame God, do so. God has very broad shoulders, and God has the ability to see into your hearts, and know where you are coming from, and he has Infinite Love and Infinite Patience. If you decide that you are going to be angry at God for years and years, I promise you, He will out-wait you, and he will love you every moment on your journey until you are ready again to deal with Him, to forgive yourself for being where you were with regard to Him, to begin trusting Him again.

Hate the other person if you must. Hate yourself if you wish. Be angry. Deny that this happened. Cry. [Crying is one of the most powerful tools that you have. It gets the energy outside of you. Every tear carries a particle of negative, unhappy energy outside of you—so that it can be released, so that it can be evaporated, so that it can be dissolved—and takes with it that tiny bit of negativity.] So cry copious tears. It helps. It works.

When you go through all of the grieving process—the bargaining, "I'll do this if you only let this situation revert to goodness. I'll do this if you'll only let me have this." Try all the bargaining you want. Hate whomever you must—the only thing that we urge you to do is not stay there, but even that we have much patience for; even that we will love you for; even that we will give you, time and time again, opportunities and challenges to change that.

You are a living, growing, breathing, changing particle of Divine Love, and we know, even if you do not know, that you have the ability to transcend this, to go beyond this, and we can be patient. If you hold a negative point in your Life until the end of your days on earth; we're still there, loving you and ready to help you with Forgiveness, even after this Life.

Forgiveness—we have reiterated—moves you to the State of Grace. All karma can be dissolved through the application of the Law of Grace. By saying, when you come into a situation, "I could respond in this way, but I choose to respond in a higher, more gracious, more loving manner"—You may have been involved in a situation, and every single one of you has been in a situation where you have treated another very, very badly.

Nobody gets through their many thousands of Lifetimes without having opportunities to hit back and to be the very worst expression of who they are. You also get the opportunity to be the very best expression of who you are.

It's all your choice, but having said that, when you come to understanding that you are brought to a person to balance the karma between you . . . Perhaps they hit you in another Life, and you have the choice to hit back. That balances karma, so go ahead and hit back, but they might rear up in their anger and hit you back. Now where are you?

This is escalating the war. We will say to you, if you say, in any situation with another person, "I could do this, but I choose to forgive us both. I choose to say, 'I won't hit. I want peace between us. I will let this go for the Greater Good of both of us.'"—that is the Law of Grace in action, and you are released from the situation.

If, in the meantime, they are spoiling for a fight and want to hit anyway, that is up to them, but when they next need a lesson in Grace, in Forgiveness, or in how to balance a karmic situation, they will have someone different to deal with, because you have transcended the situation, and you have transcended the person. And so, you will meet someone who vibrates according to your new vibration, your grace-filled, loving vibration. Do you want to meet them again?

Your choice, as is all in your Life. Know, My Loves that however you choose to meet the circumstances of your Life, The Divine and we say to you, "As you wish". If your belief in Life is destructive, dangerous, frustrating, stressful, then we say to you, "as you wish," and you experience stress, danger, destruction, et cetera, but if you have the confidence and if you have the awareness and the belief in a loving God—and know that every circumstance in your Life is for your benefit, that every situation that you meet is there to help you, and support you, and allow you to feel all The Divine wants for you, which is always your Greatest Good—then that is what you will meet.

You will have no issues with abundance because you will have already counted all the blades of grass in a square foot of lawn, and you know that abundance is the rule. The human perception of lack is the exception. When you agree and choose a positive experience—step-by-step, breath by breath, and moment by moment—that is what you experience. When you understand that every breath that you take is for now and in your future, then you experience a depth and a richness in that breathing, in that Life experience, that allows you to move into a future that sustains you, fulfills you, and brings you to a Life of great delight.

It is all, My Loves, "as you wish," and your willingness to move beyond where you are, in a loving manner, leads you to the results that bring you the Greatest Good, the Greatest Love, and the Greatest Joy in all that you do.

Dear hearts, Our Beloved, you have been very attentive on this somewhat challenging topic. We will say to you that by the Grace of the Most High, as you have come in, so you go forth from this place changed, and that all that you would do to forgive yourself or any other is now granted to you.

By the Grace of the Most High, you are brought to a state of Inner Peace, and, as you go forward, you have the ability to bring into you this blessing and with it Our Great Love.

My Loves, this has been a great Joy for us. We invite you to enjoy the freedom of Forgiveness in your Life, and we would remind you that *butterfly* is the symbol of this freedom. Be blessed My Loves, and remember that we love you.

Namasté, My Beloveds, indeed.

# CHAPTER III

# Celebration

In this gathering, the Archangels Gabriel, Raphael, and Michael were joined by Metatron to share their uplifting messages about "Celebration." and how we can enhance our Lives by commemorating each experience and the potential it brings.

Archangel Gabriel speaks on joining head and heart to blend mind and emotion through celebrating Life's circumstances.

From Archangel Raphael comes a reminder that Healing through Celebration is a wonder-full way of uplifting attitudes and expectations and, therefore, the momentum to heal through the positiveness that celebration brings.

Metatron's presentation on Celebrating All Life Everywhere is also about realizing that Life exists everywhere in everything and when even one part of Life is rejoiced in, all Life is blessed.

In acknowledging that all of Life is joined and unified as a magnificent creation, the Archangel Michael encourages not only celebrating this but also rejoicing in it moment-by-moment.

If a condition, circumstance or event is worth being in your life, it is worth enjoying; and if it is worth enjoying, its worth celebrating too.

# Talk to Your Heart—Archangel Gabriel

Wonderful Beings of Light, with great delight we come together to celebrate with you; celebrate the moments, the joys, the sadnesses, the experiences of every day of your Life.

It is one of the major reasons why you are here, so that you can work with the energy of The Divine and understand and know that Life is meant to be a celebration, that you create holidays—you create experiences, reasons—to say we've done well; we're having fun; Life is full of meaning; Life is a great joy and a great delight. And having included that vibration in your Life, you are saying to yourselves at every moment:

> Life is indeed a great gift. It is something that I have been granted so that I can become more of who I desire to be, so that I can learn and expand and extend myself in a very joyful and dynamic manner, so that I can go beyond any situation that I am in, and know by my celebrations that I am marking and acknowledging my progress, my successes, my great delight in Life.

This is a way of talking to yourself. This is a way of communicating how positive things can be, how amazingly de-Light-full things can be for you in every moment, and as you take the time to celebrate each and every day, you give yourself encouragement, not only for that day, but for the next day as well, so that your ever present Now-time is, indeed, filled with moment after moment of amazing Joy in your Life. When you celebrate an event, when you celebrate a harmonic, when you celebrate an experience that you have had or an awakening or an understanding, you are enriching your Life.

You are saying, "The reason I am here is of great worth, great value. I'm doing very well. Now it's time to have a party." And so, you go about this, and you celebrate this.

But some of you will say, "Well, Life is not so great day after day after day," but I promise you, My Loves, if you look for it, there is always a silver lining in every cloud. There is always a positive benefit in every circumstance, good, bad, or indifferent. It cannot be otherwise. The circumstances that you undergo were created in consultation with The Divine and your Guides and Guardians to be of service to you, to benefit you, to allow you to grow beyond where you are at this point, to bring you closer to The Divine and The Divine is unremitting Joy.

Therefore, if there is nothing to celebrate, you put yourself in a position of separation, of distance, from that ongoing, ever-present Joyfulness. You are not looking at yourself or your Life from the standpoint of Love and kindness. And so, if from time to time you tend to engage in Random Acts of Kindness, then My Friends, My Dear Wonderful Ones, give that Random Act of Kindness to yourself.

And when we say "random," we do not mean "occasional." We are encouraging you to engage in this kind of activity every single day. Random may be the direction in which you shoot that kindness and even gifting it to yourself, but it is not random in the timing of its occurrence.

If you wish your results and your positiveness and your reasons for celebration to be once a month, then so be it, but if you wish to have a Life that is filled with reasons to celebrate, with Joy, with happiness, with purpose, with service, with compassion, with Love, with understanding, then you need to allow and work with that energy every single day. It does not have to be time-consuming. Many of you worry about, "Oh dear, one more thing on my To Do List that already has 468 things on it," and that is not our purpose here.

Celebrate the fact that you have a very long To Do List. At the very least, it will keep you from becoming bored with your Life as you check off this, and check off this, and check off this.

My Dear, Wonderful Ones, celebration is the way that you talk to your heart. Celebration is the way that you make moments and intensify the experiences of your Life so that you are creating a history of positive dynamic. When you celebrate one occasion—the fact that you finally got it into your head how this program works and now, if not an expert, at the very least, you are comfortable with it—celebrate that.

This is a milestone.

This is an accomplishment.

This is something worth celebrating.

If you stumble and bash your toe and scrape your knee and are not able to rush around so busily for the rest of the day and maybe two days after that, celebrate the fact that you didn't have to break your neck to get a rest. It is called looking on the Bright Side.

But I say to you, when you get in the habit of it, you will discover that there is only a Bright Side.

Once in awhile, as you look up at the sky, you will see the clouds are very, very dark, but oh, how beautifully the light patch looks against that darkness. It is how you choose to experience your Life. Celebration toasts every event in your Life, and yes, it is true, into every Life comes difficulty, into every Life comes sadness, and even these need to be acknowledged.

There are many people who, experiencing the transition of an individual, go into stages of mourning that last days, weeks, months, sometimes even years, and we would encourage that they look on this situation as an opportunity to celebrate. There are those who have taken on the understanding, most strongly demonstrated through the Irish and their traditions of a wake or a gathering together and a conversing, a sharing, a celebration, an acknowledgment of the impact that this person had, remembering the times that you made each other laugh, remembering the times that there was some degree of assistance, something good about the Life of this person. It is there to be celebrated.

The mourning is not for the person who has departed. Face it, My Loves, the mourning is for you feeling left behind, feeling that these people have gone from your lives when, in actuality, they are more alive than you are, and so you can celebrate for them, and you can celebrate for yourself, that that Life that you found so valuable has only changed form. It has not been lost.

And, as you understand that, allow yourself to go through the grieving process, of course. When you have a traumatic illness, allow yourself to be angry about it, and to be disturbed about it, and be depressed about it, but don't stay there. Know that there's something of benefit in this. Somewhere there is always a sparkle, a gain, or benefit, for any circumstance.

This is a promise, and it is not my promise, My Loved Ones. This is the promise of The Divine from whom all Goodness comes.

When you awaken on a chilly winter morning and you think, "Oh, I don't want to have to get up—its cold in my room—and I have to go outside in the snow—and it's cold out there . . ." Understand that at that moment you can celebrate the warmth of the bed that you have, and you can find other ways and means of celebrating that day; find a good friend; go for a walk in the snow; start a snowball fight. Make it a tradition, but find ways and means of signalling to yourself that at this moment—which is the only moment that exists—Life is worthwhile.

There are individuals among you who will say, "For Heaven's sake, don't stick your tongue out and catch snow flakes on your tongue. Its acid snow just like we have acid rain and it will cause your body harm." And I will say to you, My Love, if you accept that as a Truth, then you will have that experience.

You can celebrate the fact that you have made someone else an authority in your Life, and now, knowing that, you have the opportunity to make yourself the authority by saying, "I choose that that is not true for me," and you let it go. You reaffirm over and over, "Snow is a wonderful gift, and snowflakes on the tongue tickle me. I will enjoy this experience," and so you do.

I say to you that there are many circumstances identified or judged as negative that when you turn them upside down, when you step back and look at them from a different perspective, you can understand that there is value here. There is positiveness here. There is a great benefit here.

One of the things that we will encourage you: there has been a great deal of talk in the media about bird flu, and how the countries of the world must work very hard to prepare for the coming pandemic that will be started and will be generated by bird flu, and whenever this is discovered in one bird, whole flocks are mown down. And it is thrown in the media again, and the drug companies say, "We cannot guarantee that there will be enough vaccine by the time the pandemic comes for everyone who is going to need it."

What are they saying?

They are saying, "Go into fear," but what we are saying is that, in the course of all of this flu epidemic that they are talking about, there has been less than 300 human lives lost out of 6 billion, and when you look at that . . . sadness, yes, for those lives, but those lives are saying to you, "Look at the real situation. Know that it is being blown out of proportion. Take responsibility for whether or not you are going to move into fear and panic and generate an expanded potential for this pandemic to occur, or are you going to say, 'I choose not to have this experience. I choose not to panic. I choose not to be worried about whether there is enough vaccine for me or not because I have chosen that I will not need it.'"

And so, you armour yourself, and you strengthen yourself. You are making this choice out of empowering yourself. You are not falling prey to fearfulness and exaggeration. And so, when this comes to your attention, and you take a look at the wholeness of the picture, and you say, "Less than 300 who have made their transition in comparison to more than 6 billion. What is the panic here? Why is everyone going off the deep end? What is the benefit in this for me?" And the benefit for you is that you are aware there is no need to panic.

So you can go dance in the streets, party around, celebrate your level of awareness, and with that celebration, with that positive energy, you are armouring yourselves. You are strengthening yourselves. You are filling yourselves with a great deal of power to reflect back to The Source whatever negative, fear-filled vibration is being sent towards you. When you look on your Life to find reasons to celebrate, you will always have the opportunity to find more reasons and to have more celebrations.

It is a matter . . . as we have told you many times . . . Where is your focus, and having your focus on this situation or this one which brings you greater joy, which makes you feel more comfortable, which is the one that you really want to have as part of your Life? And when you choose the radiantly happy one, rather than the fear-filled, depressing one, that is a reason to celebrate.

And even if you allow yourself to be caught up in that fear at the moment, understanding that every day you get to choose again: "What am I going to celebrate today?" That gives you a new page, a new opportunity to move out of fear and negativity. So you can, indeed, celebrate the circumstances of your Life. It's why you have a Life.

You don't have a Life to go through trials and tribulations, to experience them, to have them knock you down over and over. You have these experiences to transcend them, to go from where you are to the Higher Potential, and celebrating helps you do that.

It is a very positive energy. It is the kind of energy that builds on itself, so that when you celebrate one thing one day, the next day, when you celebrate a second thing, it is not addition. It is not even multiplication. It is logarithmic expansion, and it keeps on expanding and expanding until you stand arms outstretched, as a Figure of Joy, receiving and celebrating, moment by moment.

Dear Ones, we challenge you, "Find a reason to celebrate." There is a website that you can go to. It is a calendar website that talks about celebrations and will give you celebrations from cultures throughout the world, for every single day of the year. If you don't have a reason today for celebrating, there's sure to be one there that you can adopt for the day and expand your vision and your experience. Celebration is about making your Life more: more bountiful, more radiant, more exciting, more fulfilled. And so, I raise my glass, and I say to your celebration, long may it reign.

# Heal through Celebration—Archangel Raphael

Gentle Beings and Dear Hearts, we are speaking this evening of Celebration, and I wish you to know that celebration and all the energies that participate in that type of an event are created and are intended to bring forward healing at every level.

When you celebrate the physical circumstances of your Life, it heals any lack that you have in your Life. It looks after your wanting and moves you to considering what you would desire. It heals the gaps in the flow of abundance, in the flow of any physical need, in the Life pattern. As you celebrate, it brings forward the vibration of gratitude: gratitude for a Life, gratitude for an understanding, gratitude for a compassionate heart, gratitude for success—however, you define your success, gratitude for the beauty in the physical realm but also gratitude for the beauty in other realms of your Life. Celebration is an acknowledgment, not only of The Divine in your Life, but the purposefulness of your Life, the progress of your Life, the ability that each of you has to make your Life more worthwhile, more beautiful, more comfortable.

Celebration has a mental effect as well. This is why, very often, when you see the colours of celebration, what you are seeing, very frequently, is the colour yellow, and in that capacity it touches the mental modality with the concept of Joy, for that is the colour of Joy. It is also the colour of career, and we would have you ponder that positioning of joy and career as being the same vibratory colour. If you do not have joy in your career, can you celebrate the fact of desiring or intending a career so that it becomes a joyous experience? If you do not have joy in your career, can you make an adjustment that will make it more joy-filled? It is something to ponder.

Celebration is the vibration that heals the heart. It allows you not only to understand that your Life is worthwhile, but it allows you to know that you are even more worthwhile. You are not your Life. As in your career, you are not what you do. You are not who you declare or label yourself to be. You are not your accomplishments. You are not your successes. You are a Divine Child of a Loving Creator, and that, in and of itself, is something to celebrate.

And you have been given the gift, not given to everyone, but you have been given the gift of accelerating your growth and your understanding of Life as it can be, of yourself as you can evolve to, or rather open up to. You can experience The Divine Creativity within you in a more dynamic manner by going through the experiences of this Life. You are not in this Life to pay back old debts. You are in this Life to heal old wounds and find ways of expressing "De-light," and if you look at the word, you will understand that it means *Of the Light*. That is who you are. You are Of the Light. And so there is Joy. "Celebrate" itself means to make known, to express the Joy that lives within you, and when you do that, in positive ways, in uplifting ways, in sharing ways, all who are touched by that vibration are also moved one step further to their own healing.

The emotional concept of celebration puts a whole new spin on the experiences of your Life. When you look at Life as a Great Joy, when you say . . .

> I choose to be happy, and I choose to express it in tiny little whispers and in great big, huge, radiant celebrations. I choose to let everyone know how great my Life is, not to put them down but to let them know that Life can be so enormously de-Light-full, so gigantically wonderful, that they are going to want to say, 'Either that person is totally crazy, or they have something I want.'

And as our wonderful friend, Leo Buscaglia, used to say,

> If your neighbours think you're crazy, that gives you a huge latitude for behaviour. You can get away with a great deal, and all they'll say is, 'Oh that's that crazy Buscaglia. What can you expect,'

And there is no judgment in that, but it gives you all sorts of room to express your unique and fun point of view about Life.

When you express your interest in Life, when you express the point of view that Life is worth participating in, from the manner of celebration, from the manner of toasting it and going beyond ordinary, when you colour it with radiant splashes, it becomes more intense. It becomes more uplifting, and I say to you that energies like Celebration and Joy cannot be contained. They must be expressed. They must bubble out of you. They must make their impact.

And so it is that when we move into this physical body of the Channel, there is a bubbling up of our Joy and hers in the laughter that is often heard. This is the healing part of celebration. Celebration connects you with your High-Self, connects you with your Soul energy and makes an interactive flowing pathway for your Guides and Guardians to bring to you more successes, more positiveness about yourself, more understanding at a very deep, non-verbal level of how to continue and continue and continue to work with that flow.

When you are in The Zone, as some say, when you are in the stream or in the flow, as our friend Abraham says, then, indeed, Life rolls on in a very positive way, merrily, merrily, merrily. Life becomes even more worthwhile than your mind tells you it should be, or than your heart tells you it could be. It becomes a fact.

Now, celebration is not about chasing experience and going from one to another to another to another, always searching for something that's going to hype you up a little bit more—that is not about celebration. Celebration is acknowledging that there is a piece of goodness in your Life, and whether that goodness acknowledges a personal success, whether that goodness acknowledges some force or Being or Life around you, that made you take notice of how delightful or intriguing it was, that is what celebration is about, and, of course, it need not be made a great point of, but celebration never hurts, in any form.

When you share your de-Light in Life, others are automatically uplifted in their vibration. It is an irresistible vibration. When you let out that Joy-full-ness, when you fill yourself up with so much happiness that it must be radiated from you or you feel you will burst, you are uplifting the vibratory field of every individual that you come in contact with, vibratorily, and it affects them in such a manner that their uplifted energy touches others and touches others and touches others until it is a global, expansive increase in positive energy, and there are always situations to celebrate. The determination of the race of humanity to expand peace, to experience Life as a love situation, has assisted in uplifting the global vibration to above a Life enhancing level.

Up until 1980 the vibration of all the Beings on the planet was not at a Life enhancing level and had not been for centuries. Those individuals on the planet, who were vibrating above the level of Truth and integrity, were able to counterbalance the many hundreds of thousands and millions who were not at that level, but the job has become easier because the race as a whole, through the work of many individuals choosing love, choosing peace, seeking to have more equality and more respect for each other and to share and express that, has shifted the vibration, and the vibration on the planet now resonates several points above the demarcation of Life enhancement, of Truth and integrity, and I say to you that that was a great healing work, that each and every one of you here present, in hearing these words, is able to take some degree of responsibility for it.

By attempting on a regular basis to look at Life as a wonderful thing, as a creation of your own, as a work of art and beauty, and by celebrating that, acknowledging that, expecting that this will increase, and doing moment-by-moment what you can to bring that vibration into a richer state, each of you has helped the planet grow beyond where she was, and the peoples of the Earth to grow beyond where they were.

This is a magnificent work and worthy of your celebration. The individual known as Louise Hay has crafted and channelled a great many affirmations to assist individuals with dis-eased states within them, to re-format and re-create them in a very positive way. And I say to you that it is this type of work that is to be celebrated. When you look at what is wrong within your physical construct and move beyond that to what you need to hear, to know, to take in as your experience, the rightness of it, the lovingness of it, the healing-ness of it, then you can move into celebration energy, and you do not need to be in this dis-eased, upset, disharmonious vibration.

Because you have that guidance, it is worthwhile knowing that a particular physical condition has a reason that it speaks to you, and once you know this reason and are able to move to the positive side of that reason, then there is another expanded opportunity for celebration. You know that you don't have to stay in this state any more because the way out has been shown to you in a very simple manner, in a very rhythmic manner, in a manner that is pure enough and simple enough that you can memorize it and go beyond where you have been.

Celebration heals hearts, we have said, and, therefore, it is an important part of mourning, but celebration also, like the words "excellent" and "wonder-full", has responses to the conditions of your Life, that allow you to move upward. It is uplifting energy. It is upward moving energy.

And I wish you to know that when you are at a state where you wish to say . . . [Where] someone says to you, "How are you feeling?" and you say, "Surviving," know that that does not mean that you have your recommended daily allotment of vitamins and minerals. It means your chin is an inch off the floor which is where those recommended daily allotments will put you.

But when you say, "I'm excellent," when you say, "I'm wonder-full," not only will you shock them into considering that they might like to go there too, what you are saying to your Life is . . .

> I'm strong. I'm uplifted. I'm going beyond—survival, well okay fine—but I have a brightness in my Spirit that wants me more than an

inch off the ground. I'm going to stand up. I'm going to raise my chin. I'm going to accept the challenge because problems wear you down, but challenges lift you up.

And so, celebrate even your challenges. They are in your Life so that you can transcend them. They are in your Life so that you can become stronger. They are in your Life to assist and facilitate your choices towards Love, Harmony and Happiness. It is very much worthwhile of your attention.

And when you find that you are becoming caught in the cycle of unhappiness, the place where you cannot see any glimmer of light, that not only can you not see the light at the end of the tunnel, but you don't even know if there is an end to the tunnel—you've been in this cave for as long as you can remember—and at that point what you need is self-nurturing.

At that point what you need is to love yourself as you would if you were expressing your love to The Divine, to your partner and lover, to your child, to your parent, imagining what you would do in that circumstance for another—please do remember that to imagine is to make an image, and so you make an image in your Body, Mind, and Spirit of what it would be like for you to feel cared for and cared about, and that is your first step toward healing, that is your first step away from despair, dis-ease, that is your first step towards celebration, and that step is worthy of celebration in and of itself.

Beautiful Ones, if you could see yourselves as we see you, indeed, you would understand why we say: you, exactly as you are—poised on the brink of new self-awareness, moving away from who you have been, moving toward who you can be, and choose to be—are in the most empowered position, moment by moment, because each new moment gives you the opportunity to choose again.

You do not have to stay where you are, unless of course you're at a party, and you're trying to continue celebrating. Indeed, celebrate with great exuberance, and you will find that that exuberance returns to you very much multiplied.

# Celebrating All Life Everywhere—Metatron

Divine Lights of The One Light, I bring you greetings.

It is to some, perhaps, a strangeness that I pretend to give a vibration that is fairly solid perhaps, solemn perhaps, should be speaking to you on this occasion of the vibration known as celebration, but I wish you to know that having viewed the Akashic Records of many, many thousands of incarnations of many, many Souls, it is extremely apparent that these individuals, incarnated into the human configuration, have for a very long time misinterpreted the point of Life, and this is why so many have had to deal with the repercussions of that misinterpretation.

When one celebrates Life and the events in Life, it is done to empower the next stage of their Life experience, to look at the circumstance, to find the good in the circumstance and take that, like a priceless seed with which you plant in your heart the potential of moving into a newer, brighter, more growth-enhanced space and become more of who you are, but you leave behind the husk and the old circumstance so that it is not necessary to re-create the same instance over and over. Indeed, as you take each opportunity to view a situation, evaluate it—not judge it—and find the potential for expanded growth within it, you are, in essence, adding to the complexity and the purposefulness of yourself so that you can grow more, not in physicality, but in spirituality, to become more and more aware of the God-likeness of who you are and more and more aware of the joining, rather of the Unity.

It is not a matter of bringing two separate Being-nesses together but to become aware that within thyself The Divine already rests. When you acknowledge the upliftment or the accomplishment or the movement into a newer, brighter, more positive state; you are acknowledging the conjunction, the participation in Life, of Divinity within each of your lives.

You are opening up to the understanding that you cannot and never have been separate from Divinity, but that you are part-and-parcel of Divinity, as you experience those circumstances, those people, those occasions, that allow you to be aware of the Goodness of your Life, of the upliftment and the positiveness that lies scattered around you, waiting like apples on the ground to be picked up, lowering itself to you like apples in a laden tree to be plucked off as you understand that this is available to you, and yet you have shut your eyes.

When you reach, when you ask, it is always given. When you expect that Life will be a party, when you expect that there is always a reason or a purpose or an upliftment in your celebration of Life, then you come to know truly the reasons why you have incarnated. You have been created by Love, for Love, and through Love to experience and radiate that Love, through the choice of happiness and the manifestation of Joy. Are these not reasons to celebrate?

You once thought so, and as you choose to put your focus on this kind of positiveness, you will, indeed, come to understand that that is, indeed, a valid, a positive, a de-Light-full reason and yet we will carry you beyond reason. We will carry you to the intuition of Life's circumstances. Each of you has a strong and dynamic understanding of what Life can be, of how the circumstances in your Life are not necessarily what you would have chosen, and yet, although you do not always understand how to go from where you are to where you desire to be; nonetheless, there is an awareness that on a certain day, in a certain circumstance, this is not what you would consciously have chosen—this is not what your heart would have desired for you.

Realizing this at this moment, realizing that the situation you are in causes you greater tension or stress or disturbance, you take that gift and say to yourself, "I thought this would be wonderful for me, and it is less than I would like. Where now can I go?"

And put before you the different opportunities, the different circumstances, the different choices that you could make, put before you those choices that you might consider impossible or out of your reach, put before you possibilities, potentials, dreams, visions, and see how they feel, see what it is that they would say to you.

Remember this Life is not necessarily about society's standards. It is about your own experience of Love and Joy in your Life. It is about your own experience of Joy and Wealth in your Life, and these all come together with great clarity. When you discover that your intention and your experience of positive energy—however you describe it—and your experience of a wealth of all sorts of experiences and flowing-ness in your Life, all comes from the same intention, then you are truly on the way to having an experience that allows you to celebrate over and over.

It has been likened to a party, and there are those of you who say, "But parties are such stress, and parties are so difficult to keep the energy going in," and we will say to you that anything that requires great effort is not in your stream, is not flowing for you, and maybe it is your *concept* of what a party is that needs to be re-evaluated.

You can celebrate the sound of the rain on the roof.

You can celebrate the sparkle of one shining light in the night sky through your window.

You can celebrate the mosquito that lets you know your hearing is still very good because you have heard it.

You can celebrate positive and negative situations. The one alerts you to what is not uplifting to you and gives you an open platform on which to base a new decision.

Those things that you judge to be negative may not necessarily be so, and those things that you judge to be positive may have the opportunity of becoming more so. It all depends on what you choose for yourself. We will say to you that your choice in these matters is very powerful.

We would have you know and understand that it is possible to transcend those circumstances in your Life that interfere with the desires and the intentions of your Life. For example, we cite the case of an individual who, beginning to explore the spiritual realm and the metaphysical world, found it of great interest and great importance to spend time with individuals who had awareness of these, to her, new teachings, and the great desire that grew within her to spend time, to sit at the feet of masters, to share questions, to learn and to learn and to learn, was very important to her Life.

It felt like a great moment in the Life, and yet there was a situation that the individual had been diagnosed with an allergy to tobacco, and many of the individuals that she desired to learn from, at that time of the world, as did many, used tobacco for smoking—what is going to happen here? How can this be transcended?—This one, at one point, was taking allergy injections to alleviate the sensitivity to tobacco smoke, and yet by taking injections a week apart, every new injection was a re-exposure and an intensification of the allergy. And so the shots were stopped, but the allergy remained—what is going to happen here?—

This individual, in her growing understanding of choice and in her growing self-empowerment, in the experience of what was important in her Life, of being able to be with individuals in Joy, in the satisfaction of curiosity and the advancement of spiritual understanding, chose to be able to be with these individuals and chose to let go of the allergy because it became more important to her to have the knowledge and, therefore, transcend the circumstance that appeared to block the availability of the knowledge.

We are saying that any circumstance in your Life that seems to set up a barrier to your celebration of Life as an empowered state for yourself can, indeed, be transcended.

It is a matter of becoming emotionally connected to the positive result that you desire and thereby make that choice and move toward that exciting, stimulating result. When you celebrate, leaving behind a circumstance that interferes with your growth and your progress, you seal the door against that energy, and you move into a new space where your learning is supported and expanded, where Life can become richer, deeper, brighter and more positively played out, where you are able to experience and enhance your manifestations of those experiences that make Life more beautiful and more meaningful for you. It is a matter of what you choose and what you intend.

By understanding and joining yourself with the energy of Divinity, you do, indeed, intend a more positive result, and that opening up to the Unity that the two of you are, going beyond, coming together and understanding that you and Divinity already are together on the same team, enhances and expands the results that you are able to manifest, that you are able to create, so that you can continue to celebrate.

Those who guide you, those who watch over you, those who are the agents, as we are, of The Divine are ever available to move forward with you in identifying and in experiencing bright, crystal-pure, and delightful energies—

Joy to each of you and joy-filled celebrations.

# Celebrate the Unity—Archangel Michael

Dearly Beloved, how delightful indeed. We enjoy the opportunity to come together, but on such a topic—Celebration.

What have you celebrated today? We will get this out of the way very much at the beginning of this part of the talk. For as many of you know, thanks to the Channel and others with whom I have worked, I have a tendency of giving homework, and so we will suggest to you that whether you keep a notation in a journal in a little notebook, or in a journal on your computer, somewhere where you can access it from time to time, making a notation each day.

What is today? Is today the day that you celebrate your mother? Is today the day that you celebrate the beginning of summer, which will be the next time that we get together in this way? Is today the way or the day that you celebrate seeing your favourite bird, hearing a song that you have not heard for ever so long, and yet, very much, one that uplifts your heart?

Why are you celebrating today? That gives you your theme; that gives you your vibration; that gives you your upliftment—for the day itself.

What is it that you will celebrate today? And having done that, and having written it down, for as we tell you over and over . . .

> We understand that the human being does not like to write things down, but it does make an impression on the Universal Mind and brings things into form in a much more effective way . . .

. . . but that theme-energy, that reason for celebrating, as you review it, say every week or every month, you will see how you are creating for yourselves a history of positive events, a stream, a flow, a record, of what is worthwhile in your Life—having that theme every day.

Today, I am celebrating nature. Today, I am celebrating the fact that I tore the elbow out of my favourite shirt, and now I have the opportunity to find a new favourite. Everything can be a reason to celebrate—the rain on a day that you didn't expect it, perhaps you had planned a picnic and now you are all huddled together inside this shelter, well, how cozy can that be?—I promise you, My Loves, we live in Joy, always.

You cannot bring up a situation that we cannot encourage or find something positive in, so you might as well give up right now because you are not going to bring depression into our state, and it is why we encourage you over and over and over to bring greater laughter, to bring greater understanding of Life as a Path to Happiness, as a path to deep, personal, physical, mental, emotional, spiritual, psychic, aetheric satisfaction, that your vibration, that your experience, is always for your Greatest Good; that everything that happens to you happens for a reason and with the purpose to serve you, not to bring you down, not to make you bump your nose when you stumble and fall but to serve you, to give you times when you are very energetically up, yes, but to give you rest periods as well when you only want to be quiet, when you only want to be alone, when you want to feel that stillness.

And even if you do bump your nose, the fact that you don't have to stay there on that floor, that you can get up and rub it, have somebody kiss it better, know that you even have a nose because you have that feeling there, for there are many others who do not.

It is all reason to celebrate. On occasion you have heard of the poem that says, "I complained because I had no shoes until I met a man who had no feet." There is always someone worse off or better off than you are so do not fill up your days with judging whether they are good, bad, or indifferent. They are a backdrop in which you create the Play of your Life.

How interesting it is that those artistic creations that are called *plays*, those performances that happen in stage, in movies, in schools, are called that, not to denigrate them, not because they are of any lesser value than other experiences in your Life, but because they are meant to be entertaining. They are meant to be fun. They are meant to take you out of the solemn state that you put yourself in on a daily basis and allow yourself to feel and to experience a different vibration, a different understanding, and if that play causes you to look at yourself and say, "Am I like that? Do I behave like that? That was a sad play, a depressing play then. What is my energy like that brought me here?"

For all of these circumstances occur so that you can know yourself better, so that you can evaluate your values, so that you can look at your beliefs and say, "Does this still serve me? I believed it once. Does it still serve me to believe it now?"

You might even find that you will say . . .

> When I was a child, I believed this, and then I became an adult, and I believed something different, and now as I move even further into my Life, I am wondering, 'Do I want to go back to that childhood belief?'

Maybe it was more fun. Maybe it allowed you to look at your Life with a greater degree of curiosity or interest. Maybe it sparked the feelings of intrigue within you. These circumstances come into your Life so that you can transcend them, so that you can go beyond where you are, so that you can become more of who you desire to be.

There are a number of celebrations called "national holidays" that allow people to come together and celebrate their purpose or their reason for gathering as a community and as a nation.

Some of these celebrations are celebrations that honour individuals for the greatness of their lives;

Some of these celebrations honour parents and grandparents, and in some countries, they also celebrate and honour the children of the country;

Some of these celebrations honour circumstances and events, honour those who have gone through war and left their lives in fighting for those things that they believed in, and yes, even those soldiers, who were conscripted, had a belief that they were fighting for;

Some of these celebrations are to honour individuals, and

Some of these celebrations are to honour much larger groups.

But all of them identify themselves as part of your personal history, even if you know of no connection whatsoever in your history or your family history. Take St. Patrick's Day, as an example: celebrating that kind of vibration, that exuberance, that coming together for luck because certain groups have always done it, because it can be fun, because it wishes positive-ness and fortune to others, is reason enough to celebrate.

Coming together in community to say, "We done good again. We're continuing on. We're going to win this. We're going to achieve." When you celebrate an event, you are not only joining with others in common unity, which is the situation that all Life on the planet has, but coming together in your family of the moment, your Family of the Heart, you identify that this is an important event, that it is positive or significant in some way. As well, not only are you identifying something that, over time, becomes part of your collective history and your individual history, but you are setting in motion a vibration that can come again, as another reason to celebrate, that links to this one and the previous one and those several over there, so that you have this Spirit, if you will, of coming together for a joy-full purpose.

When you experience this dynamic, when you participate in a celebratory fashion, yes, energy is uplifted. Yes, there is excitement. Yes, individuals step out of the strait jackets and the solemn-ness with which they greet much of their lives. They throw caution to the wind. They talk to people they don't know. They laugh. They smile. They together say, "Oooooww,"—where this fireworks goes off—it brings each of you together with those other members of your Unity. It shows to you; it demonstrates to you, that there is a common link.

Even those celebrations of the avatars of religions show that common thread. Diwali, celebrated in India, is a celebration, the Festival of Lights. There is a Jewish tradition of celebrating Hanukkah, another Festival of Lights. The Christian celebration uses, as one of its most dynamic symbols, the star, the Light of Bethlehem. It all demonstrates the Unity and the Joyousness that that Unity can bring each and every individual.

When you celebrate, whether it is by shaking hands with another person, by hugging them, by smiling at them, by congratulating them, by enjoying the moment with them, you are moving out of ego-state and into the Unity, the Oneness that all Life is. That is the great importance of celebration. It allows you to move into an energy, and I say to you, Dear Hearts, that energy is a very dynamic, uplifting energy. That energy is Angelic in its focus and in its function, when all hearts come together in a way that allows each of you to feel and know and experience the positiveness of that situation, to understand that, 'I feel good about myself and this situation, and I feel good about this other person as well because we resonate, we understand.'

The celebration of Bastille Day, the celebration of the Fourth of July, have freedom as their common element, and, therefore, there is an understanding when these types of celebrations come about—"I understand why you celebrate because I celebrate too"—and it is immaterial that the dates are 13 days apart. What is very powerful is that the celebration occurs.

A great many of you have very busy lives, and that is a positive thing until your Life becomes so busy that there is no room in your Life for your own honouring of that Life. If you are so busy and so stressed that you don't have the energy to take time out and do something that celebrates you as an individual,

That celebrates you as a Flame of Divine Light,

That celebrates you as a creative, unique individual whose presence on the planet is of great importance.

I say to you, if you were not here on the planet at this time, the balance of the universe would be upset. Do not downgrade your importance.

So, taking the time to celebrate, to acknowledge to yourself, to put yourself inside your own worthiness and say . . .

I must be worth a very great deal because I have many, many, many Angels and Guides looking after me, while I'm the only one in all of that group that is here physically incarnated. I must be special because I get to be here.

And I promise you that all of us will say, "They're gettin' it."

Yes, indeed, we would have you know and understand that every moment, every in-breath and every out-breath, we celebrate. We are delighted to be associated with you. We love, cherish, nurture, honour, and laugh with and sometimes at, the lives that you lead. We laugh because you get it. We laugh when you need to be picked up because then we have our purpose to be fulfilled.

When you hear us and follow through on our encouragement, we laugh and we celebrate because you have given us an opportunity to participate in your lives, and when you ask us in fury, in despair, in confusion, in uncertainty, we celebrate with you, and we celebrate for you because that means you are taking courageous, brave new steps on your path.

When you are angry, and you just want to *do* something, we encourage you to find something constructive to do so that that anger lifts you into a more positive vibration.

When you are unhappy, we celebrate with you because it gives us the opportunity to dry your tears, to wrap our wings around you and let you know that we are always so close to you that you cannot take a breath without our adjusting our energy around you. We are always with you.

When you are confused, we celebrate even more because that means you are about to grow, and we are on your team, and we get to grow with you.

There is always a silver lining. There is always the sun shining behind the clouds. Please take comfort in that. But even more so, push away the clouds, dust off your vision, allow yourself to see through those clouds and know that the sun shines very brightly, always, simply waiting for you to notice it.

Honour yourselves through your own personal celebrations. Those of you who work with New Moon energy and bring into your Life the supportive moon energies for manifestation, have the opportunity to celebrate that as a means of understanding how you can progress, how you can create, through that organization, that practice.

Those of you, who honour your intuition and follow your instincts, can celebrate that, and those of you who do not follow your instincts can celebrate your level of awareness when you say, "Missed it that time. I'll choose better or differently another time."

This is all about living an aware Life and deciding that that Life of Awareness will be positive, uplifting, and encouraging and a whole, great big-ball-of-fun, even if you have to borrow a young child so that you can have fun in a child-like manner. Whatever it takes, My Loves, just so long as you enjoy your lives. That is why you are here, and when you understand that the word en-joy means putting Joy into, then you will work with that energy even more spontaneously and dynamically positively.

I say to you that you are a Joy to us who guide and watch over you, and our lives are fulfilled as you come closer and closer to an on-going experience of Joy. It is an amazing place to be, and we invite you to ask for it, to choose it. It shall indeed be given, and then, My Loves, how we shall celebrate!

Dearest Ones, each of you we see moving toward a greater understanding, a greater experience, of enthusiasm and expansion. As this vibration moves towards you, we would strongly encourage each of you to discover for yourselves those activities, those theme energies, that bring you the greatest pleasure and that allow you to expand in creativity and fun; however you decide it is to be in your Life. The next two and a half years will be very, very exciting if you choose to enjoy it from the aspect of an adventure, expanding in many new ways as you go through this period. It is an adventure, indeed, to participate in Life with you, and know that each of us is available to guide your steps simply by the asking.

We love you dearly. Have fun.

# CHAPTER IV

# Commencement

At this fourth gathering, the Four Archangels: Gabriel, Raphael, and Michael with Metatron and I as their Channel introduced the excitement and growth of new beginnings through the four modalities of communication, emotion, action and presence.

The theme for this evening was given to me through the reminder of a phrase taught by Val Van De Wall, one of my greatest teachers this Life.
Everything in Life manifests through this process:

Idea
Ideal
. . .
Real

Idea—First, you have the thought or the Idea
Ideal—Second, you fall in Love with the Idea and it becomes the vision or the ideal
. . .—Then, after a suitable period of gestation, the Idea becomes . . .
Real—This is when manifestation occurs.
Each of these Wonderful Archangels took a part of this concept as their topic and developed these uplifting talks.

# Thought Begins It—Archangel Gabriel

Wonderful Beings of Light, it is I, Gabriel, who am delighted to say to you, "Do you see yourselves as we see you?"

We have called you over and over Dear, Glorious, Wondrous Beings of Light as you are, and we encourage this form of loving, supportive communication with yourself to begin now in a positive way, in a way of those beings called cheerleaders, in a way of those Beings who support, who forgive, who look upon each of you as magnificent.

Do you know anyone who thinks of you as magnificent?

We do. Indeed, we do, and, Our Loves, it is most important that you look on yourself as magnificent, as a piece of art, a work in progress, but we will say to you that there has been great progress, indeed, in all that you have done.

Are you in the right place? Absolutely!

If you had made a different choice ten or twenty years ago, would you be in the right place? Absolutely!

And so now at the summer solstice, we will invite you to understand this is an energy; this is an opening; this is a portal through which you can pass and step into a new field of endeavour, a positive place from which you can take your first steps into an expanded awareness, an expanded way of being in the world.

This is not brand-spanking new, never done before. This is more like the energy of the pages of the Tarot; where you have done foundational work. You have done some of your student energy, and if now you are at this place where we are joining you, you are taking what you have learned and polishing it, working with it in such a way that you can begin to understand and experience and draw to you a brighter, more dynamic, more richly-involved segment of your life.

You are moving into your own blooming, your own empowerment. That is what this degree of commencement is about; and one of the most important tools for having this be a time when life flourishes, and you are right there with it, developing yourself with great colour, with great vibrancy, you have the power to create that.

This is an empowering step. This is moving from perhaps some tentative understandings. This is allowing you to become more of who you choose to be, more of whom you would love yourself to be, more of whom you will support, encourage, and heal yourself to be. And as you communicate with yourself, which you do so on a subconscious level on a continuous basis—so for some of you this period of time will endeavour or will bring to you the opportunity to take a new look at the way that you have viewed your life in the past, and at the way that you have allowed life to influence, or say, or approve of you for yourself—this is the time when you can say . . .

> This experience in my childhood, while I can understand from an adult state, was not intended to hurt me; I took it as a hurtful situation. Now I need to look at that and to say that in spite of that situation, whether it was caused by something I did or did not do, whether it was caused by someone who did toward me or did not do, what I can say is that I was perfect; I was lovable; I was loved by those who Guide and Guard; I was exactly as I needed to be. There was nothing wrong with me then. There is nothing wrong with me now.

It may be that there were actions of your own, or of others, that were not the most beneficial, but that is only a moment in time where that behaviour occurred. What is important for you to discover, to remember, to remind yourself of, to repeat over and over until you got it, is that you were created from Love. You were created by Love. You were created through the Guidance, Direction, and Passion of Love, and that is all there is to it. It is not that you deserve love to be given to you necessarily. It is that you are an Emanation of Love. You are here on this plane to experience happiness. You are here on this plane to move from joy to joy, to greater joy, to bliss. That is why you are here.

That is what your subconscious does not always remember because authorities have said to you—at a time when you were vulnerable, between the ages of zero [conception] and the age of seven—the beginning of independent thought—you have had a great deal given to you, in passion, in anger, in frustration, with highly emotional wrappings, given to you by authorities when you were least able to say, "Now that might be true for you, but I don't accept it for me."

Can you imagine yourself at three or at five saying that to an angry parent?

Indeed not. But now you are at a state when you can empower yourself, when you can go back and communicate with that Child energy and say, "There was a misunderstanding. They did the best they could based on what they were taught, but they didn't understand."

Now what is necessary to heal you is for you to forgive them, to say to them, "I forgive you for not being the way I needed you to be at that point, and I forgive myself for feeling it was all my fault, whether I was told so or not."

When a young child is in a situation that is difficult or hurtful, and they feel it is all their fault, it is because they understand that they are the Creators of their Life Path, and they are the Creators of their life circumstances. What they do not always allow themselves to remember is from zero to seven, and to some degree from zero to twelve, they do not have the power to get along by themselves; and therefore, they are in the care of others, and sometimes that care is not as fulfilling as it could be.

That is a lesson to say to yourself, "That was true according to their understanding, but *I* now choose." It gives you the strength; it gives you the courage; it gives you the understanding, that you don't have to stay in that vibration; that you can begin again; that you can move into that energy of knowing you are a Creative Being, that you are a Co-creator of The Divine—not because The Divine comes along from outside of you, grabs your hand, and says, "Shake, we are being partners in this venture," but because The Divine opens up within you and says . . .

> I am here with you, together, cell by cell, thought by thought, heartbeat by heartbeat we will love our way—not your way, not my way, our way—through this Life path if you will open and allow me that level of participation.

And so that is what is needed to communicate to yourself, at the deepest level, at the richest level, and for many of you, at a repetitive level, because you have a great deal of nonsense inside you that will argue with the concept that you are Creator, that you are Love, that you are Wondrous, Magnificence, and Our Delight.

That you are deserving is another thing that interferes with taking this step forward. There is very often the feeling of—I'm not good enough. If you, as part and particle of God, are not good enough, what are you saying about the God Within, or the Goddess Within, or in truth All That Is Within? Is that Being not good enough to be acknowledged as the light, the inspiration, the joy, of your Life?

Would you withhold that Love from Divinity? No. You have been truly taught that that Divinity adores you and that it is appropriate for you to adore, as complement, as one mirror showing itself to another, as one heart beating in rhythm with another. So what you would not hold from Divinity, why would you withhold it from yourself?

Now there are situations, it is true, where life has been difficult and you have said, "I want nothing to do with the God of my Understanding. I have been hurt, and I can lay no blame but on that doorstep. I turn away; you are out of my life."

And that would be fine if Divinity were outside of you, but Divinity is within, and Divinity understands your hurt. Indeed, often far more than you might understand your hurt, and Divinity is patient—unbelievably patient. If it were not so, stars would come into existence and come to the end of their lifetime instantaneously. Why create a lifespan of billions of years if you are not patient enough to watch how All Life Everywhere can evolve in that span of time?

Why come from eternity and inspire eternity within each of you if there was no patience? You have the Free Will. You can say, "I'm putting blinders on. I'm not talking to you. I don't want anything to do with you."

And that would be fine. And you will still be loved—extravagantly. And opportunities will come forward over and over and over for you to discover that there is one individual who keeps coming and wanting to do something for you; that there is a penny that falls on the ground in front of you to say there is an angel here, or a feather—that someone will do you a kindness, and you may not even know who they are. You drive up to a parking spot and there is a half hour waiting [on the meter] for you.

All of these are messages from The Divine saying, "I still love you, anyway."

Exercise your Free Will, but understand that when you feel you are separating yourself from The Divine, it is you that is doing the separation. The Divine only snuggles closer, waiting . . . waiting . . . waiting for that opportunity, waiting for that circumstance to come forward. When you hear a joke, and it strikes you so funny that you say, "Oh God," as you laugh about it; or you see something that is miraculous and amazingly beautiful, and you say, "Oh my God," or you turn in pain and you say, "God help me,"—and She is there; It is there always, whenever you are ready—no pressure—whenever you are ready.

Let this be the commencement of a new and more rich relationship between yourself and All Life Everywhere including Divinity. There is represented in your physical self some residue of All Life Everywhere on the planet. They do tell you, the scientists, that the air that was breathed-out by Shakespeare has circled the globe and is breathed-in in India and is breathed-in inside of you, that the air that vibrated when Churchill made his speeches has circled the globe and become part of who you are part of who All Life is. This is the residue; this is the resonance within of the joining of All Life, and when you can begin to understand that you are part of that deep-level form of communication, you are opening the door to understanding not only Self which is important to understand, but understanding that Life is a rich, vibrant, dynamic pattern that exists because it has something for you.

The ground that you walk on—and we are not talking of pavement, we are talking of grass and mud, and the planet herself—the ground that you walk on is there to move energy into the body, to stabilize you, to allow you to know and understand that you are safe and secure on this planet at all times, and if you will accept that teaching, you will begin to see the demonstration of its effect. When you see a flower and it takes you by surprise—you hadn't expected to see that particular flower in that particular place—or the flash of colour catches your eye, and you turn, and you see a butterfly; they are all saying to you, "Notice us; we are here to demonstrate the Vibrancy of Life. We are here to radiate forth and to share with you the experience of abundance"—not meagre abundance—but Abundance that spills all over itself and keeps coming and coming and coming as any individual who has a lawn mower and needs to make use of it can tell you. At Chichén Itzá, the temples there were hidden for many thousands of years. Why? Because the jungle grew abundantly. It is only the intellect and the separative ego that allows any of you to feel like there isn't enough anywhere.

There is enough energy in the form of food, and food materials, and those supplies that can be made into food for every individual on the planet. And yes, we do understand that is more than six billion—for every individual on the planet to live a life of gluttony if they choose but certainly a life of healthful well-being and enough every night to go to sleep with.

But because you have chosen to believe doctrines and patterns of lack that have been inundated towards you; that have been sent and repeated, and repeated; that you have accepted from the worry energy and the conditions of parents, grandparents, politicians, media—all of these have served to convince you that when you "get real" with Life—please do notice the quotation marks there—you will find that Life is not what in your heart you know it is.

Begin to live and lead with your heart, begin to question when there is a statement made, and your heart says, "If that's true, if that's true, it is regrettable. If that's true, it is an injustice; it is a wrongness."

When you understand that what you are hearing is negative, is an energy that depreciates or devalues you or any other group; sense Fear in motion and understand that that is not where Truth is. It may have been presented over and over and over to the point where the vast majority of society accepts it as true; and, therefore, it has become difficult to push your way through.

But we will remind you of the scientific evidence of the Hundredth Monkey. For those who may not have heard the story, we will quickly identify—and there have been other examples over the course of mankind's life. What has occurred is that scientists were observing a zoo where there were monkeys on an island and monkeys on the shore, and the monkeys on the island were isolated, had no means of contact to the same kind of monkeys on the shore.

Over time there came to be born a young female who took the fruit that fell in the sand on the beach and she would go over and wash it off before she ate it, and she taught this to her children, and she taught this to her grandchildren, and her children taught this to their children, and it kept going. But still that was *one* family group, and then some others on the shore would pick up the idea as well and wash the fruit before they ate it.

And then there came a day, a day that the scientists have said, "The imaginary number, the critical number, we will identify as the one hundredth monkey, and at that point, instantaneously, all the monkeys on the shore and on the island were all washing their fruit with no communication. It had come to the point of critical mass where that level of understanding simply moved its way through all of that group of intelligences, and this is what happens with what is presented into the world as Truth.

But this I say to you, you can begin something new and different. By refusing to accept, like pablum going into an open mouth, anything that you feel is not the Truth or that you would choose as not true for you—And I say, Wonderful Ones, by making that distinction, by saying . . .

> I hear what is being said, but I have not made my opinion yet. I have not voted as to whether this will be true for me in my life. I will think about this I will ponder this, but I will not entertain this any more until such time as I have made my decision.

Any newspaper report, any politician's statement, any affidavit, any court ruling, anything that is presented to you as the Truth is an opinion until you test it, and vote on it yourself, unless you simply, like an automaton, open your mouth and swallow what is being handed to you as if it were true—and this is the way to begin a new way of Being in the world, and as you do it for yourself and as you share this with others, you are empowering all of them to begin a new way of Being in the world, and this, Wonderful Ones, is how the Age of Aquarius becomes more and more present in the world. It has already begun, but it has been fighting a great many battles against old ways of looking at life, old perceptions, old hierarchies.

There have been times when it seems like negativity and war will have their way with the world. They will not. Even now there are more and more individuals seeking to live their lives from a spiritual aspect, a global, humanitarian, we're-all-in-this-together aspect, and, "I want to have a party; I want to have lots of friends. Enemies are not what I choose to engage with." Even now that energy is creeping more, and more, and more into the public consciousness. So there is hope. The new beginning has indeed already begun. The grade-school lessons are learned, and now as you come into this energy of initiation, of commencement, of re-building the way things are in your lives, you have the opportunity to re-build the way things are in life everywhere. I say to you, you are the vanguard, few though you may appear to be, nonetheless.

Your harmony with this situation becomes much more dynamic; your willingness to dare to be different, to dare to be remarkable, to realize that failure is not only not an option, it is simply an experience, like skinning your knee when you are two. Are you still there holding onto that, jumping up and down screaming and rubbing it and wanting Mummy to kiss it? It was an experience. You got over it. So too are many of the situations in your life. They are experiences. You can get over them. You can look at them in a different way.

You can say, "I'm not held there; I begin my life anew," and when you are challenged, as you will be, to take a greater depth of your life's experience, to understand more deeply how you can be the change in your life, to make yourself independent of the approval or lack thereof of other individuals, you are becoming empowered.

You are moving into the state where you can say to everyone else in the world, "You are allowed an opinion in my life, but I have the only vote." It strengthens you. There are some who will react against you because they would love to have that strength, that self-empowerment, and they don't know quite how to get it. So they will step away from you until they understand that when you empower yourself, you do so, so that you can be of service to the Greater Good. That is Aquarian. It is said to be humanitarian, but we will say it is Unitarian, to understand that All Life Everywhere, crystal, plant, animal, human, spiritual, All Life Everywhere, is one life, is one vibration, is one coming together of community. And that is the new energy that vibrates around you.

Many of you have felt recently, over the past several years, a diminishment in your energy, and that is because this vibration has been working its way in, to the Earth plane. It is higher. It is brighter. It is faster. It is clearer than what you have had to deal with before, and it takes some training. It takes some personal development within you to be able to hold this energy. And in this case, while, yes, there has been a tradition or a coming-to-understand that making a healthier body will help you operate in the world more effectively, there have also been times when you have needed to simply respect the needs of the physical vessel, perhaps by meditating, perhaps by taking up a creative activity, and perhaps simply by allowing yourself the gift of going to sleep. All of these serve to allow you to integrate this new energy. This energy has never been on the Earth plane before, not even at the heights of other civilizations such as Egypt, Atlantis, Lemuria.

Never before has energy of this clarity, of this beauty, of this effectiveness been available to the Earth peoples, and we will say to you, "Congratulations, you are indeed beginning to understand how life is truly intended to be—Love generated everywhere."

# Feeling your Way—Archangel Raphael

Dear Hearts, and so we deal with new beginnings, enhanced beginnings, and the emotional states that can either propel you forward into this or hold you back, hold you back, hold you back, until it is almost as if the Universe plants its hands in your back and gives you a long, strong push forward. The Channel is fond of saying that the Universe is not above nagging, and while we prefer to see this as on-going invitations or opportunities; nonetheless, it is an amusing way of looking at a situation.

"Dare I?"

Very often when a new opportunity is presented, when the choice of making a dramatic change or beginning something on a higher level than you have achieved before, very often it is . . .

> Dare I do this? How do I feel about it in my body? Do I have my butterflies flying in formation, or are they everywhere making me feel that life is chaotic?

For some individuals, that jittery, chaotic feeling is indeed a positive one, an exciting one, a stimulating one, and for others, it is a very frightful one. So how do you deal with it? Can change be made subtle? Can you take little baby steps into this expanded situation, or are you the kind that simply wants to close your eyes, hold your nose, and plunge in?

Each of you has an energetic modality. What we will say is choose what works for you. And I promise you that digging the heels in is not the way to work with Commencement energy. It may feel like it's the most comfortable, but it is certainly not the most effective. When you understand that the threshold upon which you stand is one that you have chosen, is one that you have written into your life contract, is designed to propel you into something that can be absolutely magnificent, then you can look at this as the potential for something good, as the potential for something much better than what you have ever had before.

Over and over the Master Teachers, the Inspirational Ones, say to you, "Choose the highest best. Choose only the very best for yourself and then follow that." We have said repeatedly over the course of the past year, "Make your choice, make your decision, based on what makes you happy."

For some, first of all, it is a matter of taking a step back and identifying what makes them happy, but even that is in Truth a step forward. It is an expansion; it is a new way of looking at life. "How do I dare to do this?"

For some individuals, beginning something, commencing something, that is of great desire and great passion in their hearts is also filled with trepidation . . .

> What am I going to do? What is my family going to do? What are those authorities in my life going to say or going to do? What will my co-workers think when I take this step? Do I need to be afraid because of deep, residual memories?

For know and understand that every experience you have ever had from your creation as a Life Force energy, through lifetime after lifetime and experience after experience, all those vibrational circumstances reside within your subconscious mind. Those who say that you only use one tenth of your brain do not have the complete picture. You use your brain indeed, wholly, because there is much more influencing you, supporting you, holding you back, and urging you forward in that depth of unconsciousness than if you were to list everything your conscious mind can remember. There is much more in that depth than all you think you know.

So at this point in Life, and in your circumstances, some of the things that you desire to do feel like they need permission, permission perhaps from another. You would not want to get in trouble again, and Lord knows you have feelings sometimes that you've been in trouble before. Yes, you have, but you have also done exceptionally well before you have faced those demons. You have transcended those dragons. You have gone forth and accomplished, achieved, succeeded. Those are the memories to latch onto, understanding that when you are filled with uncertainty, it is only saying to you, make a checklist; take this feeling that you want to move forward and look at it a little closer, not so that you can talk yourself out of it, but so you can have greater understanding of why this moment is so important for you.

This is a highly creative point in life, and it comes about every year with a new spin to it, with a new opportunity to it, with a new edge to it, so that you can work with it in a manner and in a dynamic that will fit you. It may not be that this year is your year, but sooner or later it will come to you. So practice; practice now; practice understanding that what you are experiencing here and now can be richly abundant for you, can be a star-like energy as if you are being guided, as if you are being drawn forth, as if in front of you is a space of time where you can drop the wish that you have from the deepest level of your heart, and it will be caught and placed in the sky to guide you toward that rich yearning. That is what is available here and now.

Will you look into the sky in your heart, to the sky in your dreams, and see that glowing, brilliant, vibrant energy and say, "That's mine. It's waiting for me I'm going to take the next step toward it," or are you going to close the curtains and turn your back on it and say, "I dare not?"

Either way, those who love you, those who support you, those who guide you; either way, the Divinity within you is still there loving you, supporting you, encouraging you, letting you know that you are still okay; you are still beloved; you are still supported and cherished and nurtured, and the next time that star shows up, and you feel the urge for a new beginning, that you wish to make your dreams come true, that you wish to make them real and grounded in life around, they will be there. Those who live in your heart, those who guide your steps, Divinity Within, will still be there, will still be saying, "Go for it."

We are with you every breath and every step of the way. You are never alone. Even when you are in the throes of making that decision, they are there encouraging, holding fast the energy, so that when you have the courage, when you have the stimulation, when you have the excitement to take that step and go through that portal, that solid ground is in front of you, that they are holding on to your hands, holding on to your essence, and they will fly with you. You are never alone.

What will you do?

Choices, if you look for them, will fall at your feet, will rain into your lap, will come to your attention by whatever means is necessary to give you a moment to say . . .

> Hmm, yes, this I choose. Yes, this I will dare I will fly in the face of convention. I will take the steps; I will climb the heights I do know, and I do understand, and I do trust that this that is important to me, that this that makes my heart sing, that this that makes me tingle with excitement, is mine, and I will take this step into my good, that I will follow it through.

And know that even though there are times when fear is there . . .

> And I am not sure, and I feel overwhelmed, I will understand that that is society's point of view standing in my way, but now I am choosing from a right, clear, high, and loving perspective, and that perspective says, 'I only get a dream because it's important for me to follow that dream; I only get a question because it is important for me to search

out the answer to that question; I only get an opportunity to make my life more meaning-full, more enthusiastic, more effective, more healed, more dynamic.' And so again, I am standing here; I am at the threshold. Will I turn and walk away and know that my life energy is being diminished? Will I look through the doorway at that rising sun and let it inspire me? Let it fill me with Spirit, let it bring to me an awareness that I am never more secure than when I say, 'Okay God, you're showing this to me, and I'm trusting you; I take this step I choose the danger, because only by going through what I fear, can I receive and open myself to what I would love greatly. Only by going through the fear can I open my experience to something more than whom I am at this moment, and what I can dare at this point, that only by moving through my fear can I transcend that fear and dis-empower it from ever interfering with me again. I choose the danger so that I can win over it; I choose to go beyond where I am in order to move into a wider world, a greater experience, a more dynamic, more positive, situation.'

And know that when you make that choice to expand your experience in life—when you say, "Okay, I trust that I have been brought to this point for a purpose, and I trust that that purpose is for my benefit. I will hold my breath; I will take that step forward." Know, as clearly as you have known anything ever, that that step is taken in company with all those Bright Loving Spirits who have always been on your side, cheered your path, held your hand, and who shower you with their deep, abundant, healing Love. They are within you; they surround the parts of your life around you. You are never alone unless you cut yourself off, and even then you only think you're alone, but we are with you, never separated, always together.

Allow yourself to take the step. The bridge will be there, and so shall those who Guide and Guard you. So shall we be with you . . .

# The Gestation of Peace—Metatron

Light Beings, it is I, Metatron, who brings forward the information of your individualized and participatory New Beginning, the commencement of a new way of being in your world and in your life experience. This comes about through practice, spiritual practice, indeed; and for some of you with recent memory of being at risk for your beliefs, of standing up for your values and discovering that they have brought criticism, that they have brought attack, that they have brought the cessation of life, this has brought forward the trepidation, the fear-full-ness, the uncertainty. Do I wish to walk this path?

But we will say to you, and we give you our assurance: From The Divine comes the promise, 'Never again will you be at risk for your Life's sake based on the choices you are making.'

These choices bring you further and further into the vibratory state that is Divinely Inspired. It is like coming to the understanding that what you are doing is surrounding and radiating, protecting and enveloping yourself in Iridescent Divine White Light at all times, that you are moving into this radiant, spiritual energy, and because this energy is not restricted to the Earth realm, it cannot also be influenced only by those individuals operating on the Earth realm. It requires of you the intention to begin to live your life, not only for the Highest Good of all Concerned, for a greater spiritual development, but it also requires that you live your life for your benefit, choosing your Good.

None of you who hear my words are selfish enough to say, "I will make choices that benefit me and no other, that I will expand my Good and withhold from every other." None of you are capable of doing that. There may be occasions where you will say, "No," to another individual, and then immediately allow to arise the ogre of guilt. And I will say to you and we reiterate to you, that is ineffective use of energy. If you allow the feeling of guilt to come forward, you have not been honest with yourself or the other individual about the circumstances regarding which you have said, "No."

Do clearly understand that this scenario, this response, is being engendered from a feeling that if you do something for yourself that you are taking away from another, and that cannot be. As Gabriel said, there is food enough for all mouths to be filled. There is spiritual food enough; there is independence enough; there is support enough; there is Love enough, so that if you say, "No," to one individual, you are not diminishing or taking away their good; you are only encouraging them to either create their own good or find a better fit in someone else; for them to get it from that other individual.

You are empowering yourself to respect your needs, and if that need is for you to simply take the time that they would have you give to them, and go out in your yard and lay in the grass and let the sun radiate its warmth on you; then that is what you need, and the individual or the circumstance that can respond to what they need will be brought to them. It is not up to you to sacrifice yourself for the good of the entire world. It is up to you to do what you can do to position yourself in a state of empowerment, in a state of support, in a state of lovingness, in a state of benefit, that is given first to you so that you have it to give to another. The practice is:

> At this moment when I am making this choice, can I make it with exhilaration, can I make it with grace-full Love that is unconditional toward me and this other, or must I decline in order for myself to be supported, in order for myself to experience love, to experience gratitude, to experience support, and if I can do this with honesty to myself, then there is no necessity for guilt.

We would have you understand that guilt is anger you do not feel you have a right to, and when someone asks you something and you say, "No," and the energy around them or the energy coming up from your past makes you feel bad, makes you feel guilty. It is saying to you that there is a situation here that you have not dealt with; that you are not in Grace; that you are not in Love Unconditional for yourself, because at some point you feel the obligation; you feel that you *should* have done something for someone else.

It is a situation that you need to deal with privately to release that chain from you, and so there again is the spiritual practice. What is needed when you begin something new is to set down all of those circumstances, all of those judgments, all of those scenarios, that you feel you have failed at. Lay them all down in the grass beside you, give them away to whomever will accept them, that they might use that energy for positive means; drive that energy into the planet that she might heal the situation and you by taking that burden from you.

It is a spiritual thing to come to a place where whatever you choose is supported because you have chosen it, that there is no overlay of judgment for or against you, that you are in a state of neutrality, that you are in a state of balance. When you are in this place of commencement, of new beginning, of opening yourself to an expanded potential—because that is what the summer solstice does: it takes the energies that have brought you from the spring equinox here, that have been preparation, that have been groundbreaking, that have brought you to the point where you can ask the specific questions, and now you are beginning to show the results of all that preparation you have started so very long ago—whether it was this lifetime or another.

Now you are moving into a blossoming, into an extravagant expenditure of energy, so that abundance, so that largess, can be present around you; so that your intention of creating something wonderful for yourself can begin to be demonstrated, can be manifested, and so you can take that idea that has been working deep within you and propagate it, set it down in a fashion that can be demonstrated and shown to the entire universe. This is where you take the idea that you once had and format it; shift it perhaps; re-create the design perhaps; this is where following your intuition—following the matters of your heart, the desires, the pleasures, the treasures, following what you are not sure you know but just doing what Love would inspire within you, through meditation, through contemplation, through creativity, through enjoyment of Life as it is, and the intention of creating life as it could be.

All of these are the tools that you use to bring into your life that blossoming. All the colours of the rainbow and all of their energies are available to you. The greenness with which you begin something new, coming from the heart, gives you the vitality, the stamina, the brilliance and the radiance, to make whatever you would create solid, foundational, personal growth; richly rewarding in whatever manner you see reward. It brings you to understand that this is not one beginning; this is your life from this point forward as it can be in magnificence, as it can be in potential and in possibility, as it can be when you and Divinity are aware of each other's intentions and each other's potentials for moving into a higher, greater, more expanded experience of All Life Everywhere.

When you understand that your spiritual practice will take what is within you, that Universe there, and will sing it and resonate with it to the Universe that is around you so that the two complementary, growth-oriented energies and spiritual practices blend, join, integrate, so that everywhere your life has become more, and All Life Everywhere is enhanced and more than it was before you opened to this joining and to this expansiveness.

When that occurs, it is not just about one little step in one little life. You are taking steps forward on behalf of your life as the focus but All Life as the result. You do not live life for yourself: Yes, you live life for The Divine who gave you life, but you also live life on behalf of every member of the planet. As a starting place, when you move into the potential of universal energy, when the radiant energy within you touches the radiant energy of stars around you so that the consciousness within and the consciousness of stars around you comes together for the sake of inspiration, for the sake of radiating life and radiating light into your single intention, every intention that seeks the Higher Good is also lit and inspired, and it steps forward with a greater magnificence than could have occurred if you didn't participate.

"Who, little me?" Yes, even you.

Universe, as you know when you look into your heart, means *one song*. If you do not sing your part, there is a gap; there is a missed beat, and the Great Conductor of the Universe misses you, as do all of us who listen with great joy at your toning, at your presentation, at your radiance. We miss you, so we encourage you to sing Life from the depths of your being, to let forth all of that light that is within you. Try though you might to convince yourself that this physical density is all that you are, we know the Truth. You know the Truth, and together as one, we and thee, us, in partnership, in unity, bring you that life, radiate that life, radiate that Spirit.

When you are, as you identify it—in-spired—the Spirit within you radiates forth, and you can put on as many heavy coats as you want, but it still shines forth. It still vibrates from you; it still takes one note, one word, one smile, and is placed in the heart of an individual seeking that tone, seeking that word, seeking that smile, to help them decide, will they take the next step? Will they take the next breath? Will they incarnate for the next life?

By letting yourself radiate forth with the joy, the hope, the belief, and the faith that life can be better than it was a moment ago, you are the one that inspires the next breath for All of Life; you are the one that inspires the expansion of Spirit everywhere, and you do not even know that you have that ability, that brilliance, that lovingness, simply waiting for you to go, "Open here."

Yes, all of those thoughts, all of those radiant energies, bring into manifestation the peace, the joy, the gratitude, the forgiveness, the exhilaration, the healing, the upliftment, for the race, for All the Races Everywhere, and you say, "How can I be that important?"

The Divine is within you—how can you not be that important? We know it. You may have forgotten, but you also have allowed others to take control of what you believe and distort it for their ends. It behoves you, therefore, to be discerning, to begin to check out everything that comes to you and not only say, "I choose not to agree with that," but to say, "That which I am not in harmony with I dismiss from my experience."

When you say . . .

> It is a difficulty for me to know that in Afghanistan, in Iran, and in other places of the world there are individuals who look at each other with hatred, who shoot implements of death at each other, and that is a difficulty for me I wish that were not so . . .

. . . And yet you turn around and within an hour of that you are watching a program where war happens and people kill each other. Then, there is confusion in your Universe and The Divine and those who guide you do not know truly what your intention is.

If you say, "I choose not to have an awareness of war in my life; it is not acceptable to me; I am interested in peaceful results," then, have peace in your life. If it means that you must get up and walk away from this television program that is blabbing about war, whether it be a news program, or a documentary, or an "entertainment" program, then make that choice.

Choose only love. Wayne Dyer says over and over, "Choose only love." Steve Smith, over and over, says, "Always choose happiness first; choose happiness."

When you are in those vibrations, when you are in those modalities, when you have made those choices, understand that your subconscious mind is sitting there saying, "As you wish."

When you say, "My world experience says there is only peace," the subconscious mind says, "As you wish," and writes it down, and then you go and watch a movie that involves war, and your subconscious mind, observing it, says, "As you wish." And so, you experience an argument with someone else, and all of that upset and all of that warlike feeling comes forward because you have demonstrated, you have said, "This is what is acceptable to me. This is what I want more of."

If you are comfortable living in confusion, then continue, but understand that your subconscious mind is the creative energy within you, and it will give you exactly what you are focused on without argument, without judgment. It only wants an input from you, and then it will say, "As you wish," and bring it forward. So if you want peace, that is where your focus needs to be, and it is important at that point to say, "I choose not to watch this movie," and if necessary to get up and leave the room in order to make the choice that you have already said. Fighting against war only accelerates the war.

THE FOUR ARCHANGELS

Making a choice not to be engaged in war but rather to focus on peace, that is where the energy falls off and cannot sustain itself because you are not in that warlike energy. Some years ago, perhaps with tongue-in-cheek, there were many stickers, bumper stickers they are called, and one said, "What if they gave a war and no one came?"

When you choose peace and do not even allow the concept of war to enter your experience, your mind, your heart, your subconscious, then peace is what you will get. When you focus on thoughts of abundance [then] that is your experience. Over and over we say to this . . .

> Where is your focus? What are you allowing to come into your energy field? What is your environment inundated with over and over?

Even those who "fight" for good are still expressing a belief in fighting as a reality, and so that energy continues; the war against drugs is still war and still has opportunities for that energy to continue.

Do you see where we are leading you here?

Your practice, what you have in your environment, what you have in your thoughts, for each and every one of you does not need to watch what you say, you need to watch what you think—you have gone beyond your words. You know that you cannot take back what has been vocalized, but, for you, you cannot take back what you think. It is creative. You need to monitor the thoughts you put in the garden of your mind; Norman Vincent Peale has said that many, many times.

At this point forgiving and letting go of what has happened in your past, not letting it influence you from this point forward but rather saying . . .

> I choose to create these conditions in my life, and these are the ones I'm focusing on; these are the ones that I am enjoying; these are the ones I am wrapping myself up in; these are the ones that are important to me and I will entertain in practice, in environment, by consent, by silence. I will entertain only these.

And so, when you practice discernment, you are holding them up against these qualities, and you are saying . . .

> Is this true? Good, it stays. Is this peaceful? Good, it stays. Is this contributing to my vitality, my energy, and my health? Wonderful, or if not, then out it goes.

Be very sure that you are not being influenced by someone else's advertising, spelled p-r-o-p-a-g-a-n-d-a, but that you know for yourself whether you choose this particular health practice to be beneficial to you or not, if you say to yourself, "I will have this as an indulgence and feel a little bit tantalized because it has the energy of being sinful," then what are you creating?

Is it working for you? No.

You have this feeling of doing something even a little bit wrong and getting away with it, but when you say, "At this moment I choose that everything in this item will bless my body, my energy, my health, *or* if it doesn't, it will gently be removed from my system," but rather than giving the "*or*" and letting the Universe weigh this energy that you are putting into your body, back and forth, back and forth, simply say, "I bless this food, this item, this object, that I once thought of as negative or bad for me; I bless this to my body's highest use," only.

Then go ahead and your subconscious mind says, "As you wish." Now when you are making a shift from one belief system to another, your subconscious mind may argue with you, may bring up, "As you wish now; however, note that in the past you believed . . ."

And so, there will be a period of adjustment, and then you will say to your body again, "This is good for me. This is healthy for me. I choose that it be so, and I bless it with that energy," and your subconscious mind says, "As you wish." So for a while there is some repetition that is needed, but nonetheless it is part of a spiritual practice. It is working with the intention that all you will experience will be positive, uplifting, gentle, dynamic, loving, supportive, and, of course, do not forget that all of this can occur abundantly so, with ease and grace, "As you wish."

By practicing what you choose for your thoughts, by being gentle with yourself, and by connecting with Divine energy to support you when you are still learning how to shift that energy, then, indeed, do you become the energy of healing, the energy of dynamic Love in all that you do, and thus begins your new life and a new life for the world, for the planet. Thus begins the step to Ascension, the step to transcending the circumstances of the world as they are now. What you *believe* is the beginning, but beliefs can be changed. What you are moving toward is knowledge and trust. Empower yourselves and trust that every step from this point forward is sacred, guided, and highly beneficial.

# The W/Holistic Journey—Archangel Michael

Dearly Beloved, it is a great pleasure to observe and listen in to the conversation. Indeed, many valid points are being brought forward.

Century after century, the human creature has given his power away. The hopeful thing is that within the last 25 years there has been a shift in energy. There has been a shift in self-responsibility which, of course, is the ability to respond consciously to any situation, not a situation where you can blame yourself for what happened or others can blame you; but that shift is now in the process, on the side of the scale one might say, where the race as a whole is operating from the energy of life-enhancing, is operating from the energy of Truth, rather than life-diminishing and negativity as the only scenario that has power.

So, very much we applaud the work that you have done. The understanding that you have is working. It is going forth in a very effective way, for as you voice what your beliefs are, as you think about them and work with them, they do not stay within you; you are creatures of energy, and so they move forward into the world, and [in] some places around the world, they will find another thought pattern, another Being, with whom they are in harmony, with whom they resonate, and coming upon them and resonating with that other individual, it stimulates the vibration, and that person consciously becomes available to think of the situation that you have been talking or thinking about. They think about it consciously, as well. It resonates with them; it is a global upliftment that conversations such as this do have, and we are grateful, indeed, for your level of understanding.

As you express this and as you choose to empower yourself, you are creating scenarios and situations where those children such as the Indigos, the Crystals, the Rainbows, are then able to operate in an environment that is much more positive, much more dynamic, much more beneficial, for them as well as the people they are here to teach and for their cohorts, the other children who are already on the planet and not operating at their level. So, indeed, things are improving; they are getting better.

We promise you, "No matter how long it takes, the Light will win. The dawn always comes." So then, we are talking of Commencement. We are talking of beginning life anew, and it is my great pleasure to speak on taking action with regard to this, taking action Body, Mind, and Spirit, taking action *w/holistically*, with the "w" that means every area of your life is whole and, *holistically* with the "h," making this a sacred, a holy, journey because that too has its place in each life.

For some reason I have been given the reputation of assigning homework! Far be it for me to miss this opportunity to share with you practices, points of view, ways of being in the world, that will assist you in moving into a dynamically supportive energy for what you desire, for what others desire, for what is the Greater Good in all that can come forward, and so we will say this, "That at every opportunity where you have the choice to be loving, nurturing, tender, full of care for yourself, do so."

As we have said, you are energy beings. When you do that for yourself, it doesn't stop with you. It inundates; it slides; it dances; it moves; it flows; it becomes the Stream of Life existence as our friend, Abraham, will say, and when you are in this stream, Life is very much a peaceful floating from one point of good to another point of good. And so, we suggest to you, take those opportunities, whether you are meditating, whether you are writing or speaking out affirmations, whether you are walking down the street and feel like whistling because the sun is shining and Life for that moment makes you feel like you have stepped out of time and are in a place where everything is precisely perfect. And for those of you who have seen *Star Trek Insurrection*, some parts of it very negative; it is true; however . . .

> There is a place where Captain Picard and the woman that he comes to admire so greatly spend a moment frozen in time. It is a perfect moment; Time slows down; it appears as if—even though you are moving with very quiet grace as though all the noises and all the hustle and bustle of the world around you are gone; and the bird that you can see in front of you floats, flying so slowly that you can see every feather of every movement; and that perfect moment stays with you even though you come to the point of *shift*, and you are back into the world.

This is being in the Stream of Perfect Consciousness. It has happened for many, even you, and it can happen again, and as you set your intention that you are going to be in the flow of harmony, balance, and love, you can choose to move into that vibration and experience that perfect moment not for just that space in time but for all of time. This is where you learn to live in the Now but the Now as you choose it to be, the Now as you create it, and if that means you have encapsulated yourself and take yourself in a bubble, outside of linear time and experience as the world around you know it, so be it.

The sun will still shine where you are; The Divine will still be where you are, and if you choose to reach out of that moment and invite someone else in, they are coming into a sanctuary, a space of serenity, a space of brilliant, warm love to meet with you, to be healed with you, to understand that Life can be this place of serenity and this place of exhilaration. You can invite the world in there under your conditions, under your terms.

We would recommend that at every opening to your residence—and in particular to that place in your residence where you have your sanctuary, where you have a place that feels like it is the best place in the world for you—and at every entrance, whether it is window or doorway, visualize and know and trust that the Iridescent Divine Light of the Holy Spirit washes like a light-fall in that space, in that portal, over that threshold, so that every individual, yourself included, moving into that space is automatically cleansed and cleared of all the stresses, all the imbalances, all the tensions, all the fearfulness, all the negativity of the life outside that space, and they move into a space that is comforting, soothing, life-enhancing, creative and filled with pleasure and love. And that is how you teach yourself to be in that perfect moment, every moment, like being in that serene space

And when other individuals come in, they say, "How bright it is in here; how clear it is in here, I just feel so good in this place." Of course—because anything within them that was not for their Highest Good, that was out of balance, has been restored to the highest intention for those individuals at this time, and when they leave, if they choose on a conscious or subconscious level to take some of that White Light with them and carry it into their environment, that can occur. The subconscious simply says, "As you wish," and it occurs, but much more effectively, much more dynamically, than any random thought going through the human mind because this is Spirit; this is Intention; this is living the highest, most clear, most loving, possible positive Life; it is not necessary to go and find a mountain where there is no acid rain and sit there in a loin cloth pondering whatever.

It is only necessary to understand and know that moment by moment, if you choose, The Divine guides your step, guides your thoughts, guides your experience.

When you marry your will to Divine Will, it is not about giving up anything. It is about opening up brilliant, wide doorways to possibilities you have not yet dreamed of; it is not about limitation—if I give up my will, if I surrender, I lose—it is about understanding and then experiencing that you win a vast treasure much more than you ever might have thought possible. This is about abundance that is so lavish that Scrooge McDuck would be envious; this is about Joy in Life that goes so much beyond singing at the top of a mountain because you cannot contain it within you; this is about creativity that flows from your heart and from your mind and inspires you as it inspires every other; this is about having a dream and knowing without any shred of doubt that that dream is perfect for you because you have it, and not only is it perfect for you, but it is entirely within your power to make this dream come true. It wouldn't be a dream of yours if it wasn't rightfully yours to create, if it wasn't rightfully yours to have and hold and experience.

This is about understanding that when you give your life over to God, Goddess, All That Is, it is like paying a penny for everything you ever wanted, and if you don't have that penny, it is about being given the penny so that you can have anything you ever wanted. The only condition is that it fulfills you, but because Free Will is in operation, if you choose to dream dreams that diminish you, that cause you to have to pay for your sins, imaginary or otherwise, the sins of the world, then so be it: "As you wish."

However, we feel it is much more fun, much more pleasurable, much more entertaining, and certainly a lot more to be valued to choose those experiences that let you know how beautiful you are, how magical you are, how powerful you are, how loving you are, how worthwhile you are, how deserving you are. We know who you are; we know without any question what you are capable of. Michelangelo once said, "The saddest thing is to see a man with a mediocre goal who attains it." So let your goals, let your dreams, let your desires, for yourself and All Life Everywhere be magnificent.

Does that make them any less attainable? Absolutely not!

It takes no more energy to create a penny falling on the ground in front of you than it takes to make a nickel, or a toonie, or a bag full of whatever it is you identify as abundance. It takes no more effort. When you allow yourself to believe that if you want more, you are going to have to pay more for it, whether in energy, in cash, in labour, in time—think of these restrictions—and know that that is the old understanding; that is the old paradigm; that is not necessarily the Truth for you at this point in time, unless with your Free Will, you choose to pull back out of the past, out of the old way of being in the world, and plop it in front of you and say . . .

> I'm going to bring this intensity, this major effort, this four letter word *work,* into my present and keep it to me because I've always chosen to believe that everything I earn in life, I earn through hard work. And even though I have the opportunity to make my life play, to know and understand that if I choose to sit back on a hill, watch kittens play, play a harp, and know that everything I want in my life is about to manifest

for me while I'm doing that, even though I realize I could do that, I'm still going to bring this hard work effort into me.

"As you wish."

However, the advice that we would have is to make your life a picnic where you can, indeed, stretch out in the grass, enjoy the sunshine, tease the kittens, play your music, dance to your life, have fun with it.

Do you not understand that fun was created so that you could enjoy your life; that Laughter is the second most common vibration in Heaven, next to Love, because it is that valuable; it is that dynamic; it is that wonderful.

Every time we move into this body, laughter occurs. It has never been clear to the Channel whether it is her laughter or ours, but we will say, that in the spirit of partnership, in the spirit of Love that we have come *together;* it is *our* laughter—angelic and physical. It is brought to lighten the load, because when the load becomes lighter, burdens disappear. When you understand that you are here to experience happiness, that you are here to express love, that you are here to assist in the development, the evolvement, and the healing of every individual who comes toward you in your entire life, that these scenarios were set up, as were you, to experience them and say, "Okay, June 21, 2006, lesson 478 for this year, I am going to experience this,"

Your response is going to be, "Agh, so much more work on my ever overloaded pile,"

Or "Hmmm . . . that looks like it might be fun I'll do it,"

Or . . .

> That looks like it's adding one more thing to my plate; I'm very happy with this little bit that I have here, God, would you look after this for me, please and thank you. Usual deal, I won't harass you—I just have faith in you.

And away you go, and you look after what's fun for you to look after; you look after what is rewarding for you to look after; you dance through your Life and God looks after the details. After all, He is so much more practiced, experienced, and happy to look after the details in your life than you are and when you understand that there are occasions when, having turned something over to The Divine for His tender care, someone shows up with exactly the talent, skill, and ability that you need, that is God saying . . .

Here, I'm looking after it. Let this person help; you give them a benefit by giving them something to do; they give you a benefit by looking after something you have chosen not to involve yourself with. Have fun you two!

And Life goes on . . .

Can you begin your life that way? Can you make the commitment to understanding that this is the way your life can be? Can you learn to trust The Divine? Yes, yes, yes—we know—you say that you have faith in the God of your understanding; you say that you trust by turning your life over to The Divine, that you will be looked after in a magnificent way, and yet when you do that you say . . .

> Okay God, I'll trust you. You can look after this, but I want this person to show up at this time and place for this purpose, and I want this, and I want this, and I want this, and I want this, and I want this.

Do you not have an awareness that when you turn your life over to The Divine, those things that you want for yourself are in Hands that want you to have, if not that, better; never less than—better than—that which The Divine has in mind for you is so much greater, so much more beautiful, so much Soul-, and Body-, and Mind-, and Spirit-satisfying that you could ever imagine for yourself, that the dream that you have yourself in comparison to the dream that you have from The Divine for yourself is so much different, if you could have that Trust to say, "I give my life to you; look after it and me as You will," that you are not at risk, that you are not unsafe, that you are not insecure, but that truly you have said, in essence:

> I trust that You will bless me beyond my imagining. I am open to receiving all the Good that You would give to me. I release all my suffering and all the causes of my suffering to You; knowing that having let go of it, it need never be my experience again. I have faith; I have an awareness; I trust that whatever circumstance comes into my Life that I judge to be Good, bad, or indifferent, it is there to show me how much You love me; how worthy I am of a Love that has no end and that no matter how much You love every other form of Life everywhere that does not diminish in one iota the Love that You have for me; that when You love me and my brother, it is not a dividing of Love between us but a fulfillment of all the Love in existence for both of us.

And in your consciousness of separation, that may be difficult for you to comprehend, but know, My Loves, that that is the way of it, that when from the perspective of The Divine there are two of you or six of you or six billion of you to love, that only means that there is more love available.

When you say to The Divine, "I accept everything that you wish to give me as a gift—I have this big table right in front of me, plop it right there, let's open 'em up, and let's have a party."—when you are open to receiving the Good that The Divine will give to you, it comes in big buckets; it comes in so much extravagance that there are times when you wonder how you can hold all the amazement, all the joy, all the blissfulness of it and not fly apart because you only have this physical vessel to hold that all in but the Truth of the matter is you have a Spirit of the same matter and the same consciousness as The Divine within you, and that is where all of this Amazing, Loving Essence resides.

So even though the body may feel like it will fly apart with this intensity of energy: Yes, you can hold it because it belongs to you, because it is who you are, because it is your love coming back to you. Life begins anew at this point—all of it is dealt with through the token, the coin if you will, of The Divine realm which is Love, and when you give Love away, you get more Love back, and it comes to you in the wallet of Laughter; it comes to you packaged in Joy, in Happiness.

From this point forward, this is your gift. Will you accept it? Will you open it up? Will you put it on? Will you wrap yourself with it? Will you pour it into you? Will you bathe yourself in its Radiant Light and then sprinkle drops of that radiance on the path in front of you, to every person that you meet? This is your opportunity; this is where and how you can, by working on yourself, by working on every other, move the planet and all those choosing Ascension into that higher vibration, into that loving energy.

Will The Divine do it for you? No, but He will do it through you if you are willing. And so, we say to you, My Loves, recognizing the Great God within each of you, "God willing."

Dear and Wonderful Ones, our Beloveds, you have made this evening a very enjoyable and dynamic time. Do not be faint of heart in what you are doing. Know and understand that each of you has chosen to be here at this time in order to walk through your individual doorways of self—empowerment. This is, indeed, a time of initiation for each of you. This is where you step into your new Life, your Life for your Soul and your spiritual development but understand as well, you cannot do this without affecting the world as a whole, and we, who have the honour and the great de-Light to be part of your guidance, applaud your efforts, are grateful for your courage, and salute your intentions.

Namasté.

# CHAPTER V

# Courage

Sharing their views on the manifestation of Courage, the Four Archangels seek to inspire us with forward thinking, passionate activity and heart-felt choices.

For the first time, the Archangel Gabriel speaks from the perspective of the Element of Water or Emotion when he speaks of the heart as the starting point for the expression of courage.

The usual emotional orientation of the Archangel Raphael is now grounded through the Element of Earth or the Physical nature where the healing energy of Chiron [the Wounded Healer of mythology and astrology] comes into play.

Through the Element of Fire/Inspiration, the Archangel Uriel shares the Soul's perspective of developing and living your life with courage as your muse.

The Archangel Michael develops the Element of Air by sharing the understanding of courage as a spiritual effect of one's inner communication. Making the choice of living your life from a brighter, more caring perspective not only opens your own experience but the experiences of All Life Everywhere for their blessing and benefit and your own.

# Courage is of the Heart—Archangel Gabriel

Dear and Glorious, Wonderful Beings of Light, how delightful that you have taken courage by the hand and come here to understand how courageous you are, and how you can acknowledge that and work with that energy.

Courage is dynamic action. Courage is putting yourself in a position that is not comfortable, is outside your comfort zone, but it is a growth-oriented energy. It is, in some ways, a Mars energy because it is about taking action, but I say to you, Wonderful Ones, it is not only, not limited, to that action. Courage comes from the heart. It has the word for heart in it, and so whenever you are engaged in the activity of being courageous, you are moving from the heart.

When you speak to yourself, when you work with your internal tapes subconsciously, or when you talk to yourself on a conscious level, you are always moving up and down around the issue of courage. When you are dis-couraging yourself, you are putting down, you are trampling on that heart energy, and that is a very, very challenging and difficult thing. It is not that you are talking yourself into being afraid. It is that you are limiting and holding down and stomping on the heart energy. You are interfering with your natural process.

Your natural process is to radiate heart energy—love, encouragement, support, guidance, growth. All of that is intended to radiate outward from you, but when you dis-courage yourself or any other, you are limiting that; you are putting in a plug; you are squeezing that hose, and there will be repercussions on an energetic level if you diminish the amount of Love that can tremendously travel forth from your heart chakra—that it builds up and builds up and builds up, and it must be released. If you step on this, if you hold this energy closed, if you tell yourself over and over and over that you're too weak; you're not strong enough; you're too ineffective; you're too shy; you're too . . . whatever you choose to attack yourself with . . . it will come to the point where it will either be expressed or you will find some of the circumstances in your life exploding in your face.

Do not go there, Wonderful Ones. This is the cause of many situations that are identified by the medical profession as a heart attack. It is an attack on the Heart; it is an attack on your Love; it is an attack on the balance point of your energetic self, and it comes because you try to hold yourself safe.

And so how are you going to do this? Affirmations are one thing, but affirmations, in and of themselves, do not communicate enough to you that you can, therefore, step into that positive, bright energy. When you say to yourself, "I am a beautiful, accomplished, wealthy, well educated, business person," and the Heart of you says, "Yeah right," who's going to win? The Heart of you is, because it happens at a very energized level. It comes up from your subconscious, and it is driven by emotion.

It is driven by that part of you that says, "That's not true for me." You might wish it to be. You might think in your mind it is, but until you are in alignment with your subconscious mind, until you are in alignment with the way that you and others have always talked to you, it will be difficult indeed to manifest.

We will say to you that it is important to work with affirmations, but it is important to work from them step-by-step, in little, believable increments. For example, if you were to say, "I am an internationally known writer" when you can't even get a small local magazine to publish one of your works, that is a very, very big step on your belief path; but if you were to say, "I am well known and appreciated as a writer in my community," that is not very far from where you are, and that gives you the impetus; that gives you the ability, the potential, that this could be true for you.

And so you take the courage to take one step. This is not about taking a huge leap. And understanding, that with that leap comes a great deal of trepidation, enough to block your progress. Understand and know that it takes no more courage to take that one little step to go to the local magazine and say . . .

> I've observed your magazine. I have discovered that you tend to have these themes. They are an interest of mine. What are your criteria so that I might submit?

And then working with the criteria and working with your passion—not logic—passion, you can then work on making that small step exactly what you have desired it to be, a little step of courage. While it may be difficult at first to get your butterflies flying in formation, it is absolutely within the realm of believability. It is within the realm of possibility. It is within the realm that you can understand and know you can create. And so that is how you talk with yourself to boost your courage; that is how you work with yourself in what you read, in what you think, in what you feel, in what you hear, to establish a broader definition of who you are, and what you are capable of.

There are many teachers, philosophers, Ascended Masters, and masters still in presence on the Earth plane, who will say to you, "You are a Child of The Divine," and when we say of The Divine, we are saying of the same substance, not a distant relative—of the same substance—but for many individuals that concept is so filled with awe that they cannot go there.

They would love to believe, but it is much too great a concept to accept as possible. And so then, you begin with baby steps, but you begin to know, that as a child, you will be looked after; as a child, you will be encouraged. As a child, you will be surrounded with what you need to lead you into that next step, like a grandmother with her toddler, her grandchild, holding one hand and arm behind to assist and catch that one should she fall, and watch her take the step and encourage her to take the next one. That is working with the baby steps. That is taking it small step by small step, and each time you take a step look back and see how well you have done. Know that you have expanded your boundaries, and know that you can only do that when you come from the Heart, when you are of Good Heart, when you are en-couraged.

The person that you are is in great measure your creation, the creation of yourself over many lifetimes. All of that energy resides in your deep level consciousness so that you can access it, or so that it can bring itself to your attention, according to different circumstances. The person that you are is created by those authorities in your life that were part-and-particle participants in the early stages of your Life, before you had the awareness of separateness, of individuality, of understanding that what is true for any other does not have to be true for you.

And so many of these concepts swing just below the surface of your consciousness, and when you are in a situation that another authority was in, their passion rises to the surface, and if it was positive, if it was courageous, if it took them beyond where they were to the place they wanted to be, it will take you there as well, but if it limited them, if it held them down, if it interfered with who they could be, then it will interfere with you as well, unless you have the courage to be conscious of this effect.

By using affirmations, by talking to yourself in a loving manner, you are setting the stage. It is like the script of a play that you would perform for yourself as the audience but also for yourself as the lead role. That is what affirmation is. It is the script that takes you from where you are to where you desire to be. When an actor who comes out on a stage and says the words—it is not an actor. This is about emotion. This is about feeling what you desire. This is about being passionate. Everyone has Scorpio energy. That is where your passion is. That is where your will and your drive and your determination that what you have chosen will occur, and it comes not from anger. It comes from transformation. It comes from self-empowerment.

It comes from a vast belief in the correctness and the rightness of who you are. It comes from an absolute knowing that you would not have this dream, this vision, this goal, this heart-desire, if it were not intended that you create it. And, how are you going to create it? Through the courage of your outward moving energy, through the risk-taking of gathering all that courage up and taking a breath, maybe shutting your eyes, and stepping forward.

There is a saying in many of your cultures, "The journey of a thousand steps begins with one," and that is what courage is. Courage is the step that takes you on the beginning. It is the first one, and as you go through that journey, uphill and down dale, around this corner, and into this slough and past that into this other, higher, elevated situation, the obstacles that come in allow you to know that you have completed *Courage 101* which got you started and kept the ball rolling for a while, but now it is time for that uphill climb.

Now it is time for *Courage 201*, a little bit more challenging because you have a solid foundation, a little bit richer, perhaps a little bit riskier. But when you look back on your life and say . . .

> Look at all that I've accomplished and look at the passion I have for this next step. Look at how excited I get. Look at all the energy, the feeling, the e-motion—e-motion, outward moving action.

Courage is an emotion. When you pray, it is not the words. It is not the ritual. It is the emotion, the energy that moves from deep within you to your consciousness. That is the creative factor that allows you to connect with The Divine and manifest that which you have set your heart on. Even soldiers have a goal, have a vision, have a passion, have something they have set their heart on, or they are soon cut down. When you put your heart into anything, you become very, very dynamic. You fill yourself with a solid energy that moves you beyond where you think you are capable of. This is how you knock down your walls. This is how you transcend your limits.

This is what enables you to put yourself in a situation that is uncomfortable because it is not inside your comfort zone, and thereby by going there, by being there, by existing there, and being passionate there, it allows your comfort zone to stretch, and then your arena for a positive life has just become bigger, and when you stretch out in one direction, that comfort zone doesn't become bumpy with a courage spot over here, but it is a circular energy. It expands in all directions, so that once you have been courageous enough to stand up to an authority and say, "That's not my way. I'm choosing to do this," any other authority in any other level or area or arena of your life, on that same stage, can be met because you already have the courage there, because you have already put it into place. And so that is a very dynamic thing.

Taking the step leads you into an entirely new arena. Is it a matter simply, once, of taking that deep breath, grabbing everything you can think of that is going to help you on the way, and charging into that area? Does it only have to happen once? Can you do it the first time, unlikely My Loves, but every time you take that millimetre of a step, you never ever go back to the same limited space that you were once in. It is like the stretching of an elastic band. When you stretch yourself as far as you can bear to go, even if you come to the point where you are saying, "I just can't be here any more" and zoom back to the center of your comfort zone, the edges of that comfort zone do not ever return to where they once were. They are a little further out. And so, even if you go out and have to run back, and you go out again, and you have to run back and go, "I have to get my bearings. I cannot be here. I feel too nervous. I don't know if I can do this."

And so, you rest, and you come to that stillness again, and then you say . . .

> You know, I didn't think I could go out there, but this space that I'm in is becoming so routine; I know all of it. I feel like I'm losing my energy, losing my ability to interact with the world, losing my dream, because I dare not go further

. . . And we will say to you, "Dare to be remarkable. Dare indeed to go beyond where you are." And once you feel that limit showing up again, and it feels like you have no more elbow room, like Life is losing its purpose, and so once again you gather up your courage and you say, "I just can't not try it. I must make this step." And so again you gather up your courage, you take that deep breath, you cross your fingers, you shut your eyes, and say, "Okay here I go: Charge!" and you stay out there a little longer, but you feel the tension building. You don't feel like you have that comfort.

You know that you're not as good yet as what you were in the area that you were expert in, but you're not the only one. Every person that moves into a new situation goes through the uncertainty of that learning curve goes through the trepidation of, "Will I be good enough? Can I make a success of this?"—every single individual—and maybe this time you'll stay out there a little longer, and it won't be quite so difficult, and so that is fine, and then you find, "I just have had as much as I can take right now."

And so you go back to where you are comfortable, and that is okay. Indeed, just don't stay there. Pace up and down, evaluate what you did, and why you let fear interfere with your process.

Dig up your passion again, take a look at it, post it on the wall, meditate on it. "Why is this so important to me?" And then, off you go, at it again.

Each time it becomes a little easier. Each time you are able to stay in that energy a little bit longer.

Courage is not about being without fear. Courage is acting in spite of the fear. If you are a soldier on the battlefield, and your fear is such that your weapon shakes, and you know that you'll never hit a target because it's going all over the place, grab a grenade, throw it.

Allow yourself to understand that as a child gets up on his feet and takes a step or two and goes plop onto its bottom, he may sit there a little surprised. He may cry. He may look around and see if there's an audience who's going to make it worthwhile crying, but sooner or later he gets back up again and tries it, and this time there's three steps instead of two, and this time he wobbles a bit and then goes plop, but he knows there's a good reason for going beyond.

He knows there is a positive-ness for transcending, for moving forward, for accepting that dream, and the beauty of the dream, and the importance of going past limits, gives him the courage to talk himself into it one more time.

How many chances do you get?

As many as you need, even if it is lifetime after lifetime—as many as you need—because that courage and that chance-giving and that drive to go beyond where you are, to become more, is Life energy. It is a part of your original essence, that single point of Divine spark within you desires to become more than what it is. It is why All Life Everywhere was created, so that The Creator could become more, could understand itself more, could experience more, in a myriad ways, with a level and a depth and a richness and a diversity that one single part of Divine energy can scarcely imagine.

You were created of Love to become more than who you were at the beginning, who The Divine was at the beginning. You are on a mission. You have a target. You have a plan. And all of that is to bring you forward into being outside your limits. There are those who say, "It's time to think outside the box and others who say, 'No, no, no, I would rather stay in the box.'"

As you wish, but that box will begin to feel like it's pinching you because the innate essence of your existence is to become more. All Life Everywhere shows you that; every part of the planet shows you that.

Leave a garden alone for the matter of two years and see what growth there is there; see what abundance there is there; see how it has gone from where it was and become so much more. Now some of you, with your ordered way of looking at life, will say, "Well, all it's become is weeds and chaotic, and it doesn't look good anymore. It needs to be cleaned out." But, what we are saying here is that every single plant, every single insect, every single particle of Life energy in that garden, had the desire to go beyond its limits.

Every seed has the courage to grow because the implant within it, the imprint within it, is that vision of what it could be. Every stock of wheat, every blade of quack grass, every tiny seed that will bloom one day into a violet or a cosmos or a rose has that vision, that desire within it, to become more than what it was, and you are of the same stuff. The universe expands. There are many, many galaxies that have not yet been discovered, some of which vibrate at different vibrations so that, as yet, your scientists cannot find them. Some of them vibrate in a range that science will never observe because they must be seen and believed in through the agency of the Heart and in the Spirit, but nonetheless, they are all becoming greater, more than whom they were. And having the courage to do that is an inherent part of that desire to move out from where you began.

Do you think you will find your courage? At those moments when you are most unsure, you will find it.

Can you understand and know that you have courage? You don't have to hunt around for it. Look under the bed; look behind the closet; you simply have to say . . .

> I'm open to it. I know I want to do this, and that wanting comes from deep within me. I would not have this dream, this vision, this desire, if there was not a part of me that knew how to get there, and it does not need to be difficult.

Everything, Wonderful Ones, is really very simple. It is only your intellect that tends to complicate it. Your courage will be there when you need it, when you are open to it. By realizing that and working from the mental point, the inner communication, you will be able to access it, indeed.

Step forth with Good Heart, and you will see.

# No Strings Attached—Archangel Raphael

My Dear Hearts, indeed, this courage that you speak of, this courage that you would make part of your life's existence, very much comes to you for development in this lifetime through the healing of past life circumstances.

Those occasions that you feel the greatest trepidation about are reflections or next development stages of those situations that were not completed in your past. Much of this is Chiron energy. Chiron is healing your wounds, and we will say to you that indeed it does take great courage to heal your wounds. If you were to continue to remain in a wounded state, whether wounded in the heart, wounded in behaviour, wounded in the physical form, there is so much responsibility that is not asked of you, and yet you have come here to accomplish that, to accept the responsibility, so that you can go beyond where you have ever been.

It is to be understood that this is about healing ancient interferences with the flow and the positive creativity of your life. Some of this will manifest as health issues in order that you can transcend them. Those governments who are saying to you, "You must pay for your participation in a health-care plan," are giving you the inspiration, are inspiring within you the courage to accept responsibility for your own state of health—that is the ability to respond in a positive, healing, uplifting, manner.

They may say, 'It is to save their budget.' You may feel it is one more thing on your plate, but the Soul understands that this is to give you the impetus to look at the potential imbalances, the dis-eases, the alignments and lack of alignment of a health vibration within you and say . . .

I created this. I own this, and I am reworking it. It is as if my form is a magic plastic substance that can be moulded at will. It is as if, in my child-like wonder, I take play-doh, and I make a shape, and the shape is somewhat lopsided, and the shape does not function the way I would have it, and I can do one of two things. I can take it to another, an expert, and say, 'fix this.'

The expert is now saying, "I have not the means, unless you provide me with additional energy, to fix this."

And so you say, "Out of my pocket comes the energy," and then it is fixed, but it is fixed according to that individual's standards and level of awareness, and when you get it back, you may say, "Hmmm, it's not quite the way I wanted."

So what are you going to do? Take it back to this individual and give them more energy out of your pocket when they couldn't fix it in the first place? Are you going to take it to another kind of expert and let them work with it, and they are going to say to you, "I need energy out of your pocket, and I need you to take this paint and take this scalpel or this sculpture tool and work with this and change this and uplift this."

And then you get it back and you say, "Hmmm, there's still something deep inside that is not quite the way I would like it to be." What will you do now?

At this point your Inspiration, your Higher Guidance, says . . .

> Take it to the Great Physician, take it to the Christ Consciousness, take it to Raphael, and I will help you. Take it to The Divine Itself, and say, 'There is a part within me that doesn't quite work the way I thought it would, the way I would like it to, the way I feel would be best. What is Your advice? What is Your guidance?'

And The Divine will say to you . . .

> We be partners thee and I and this is what will happen. You have asked and; therefore, we have permission. We have the ability to work with you. You have taken a great step forward, and so all that you would desire, I will give to you, that you might accept it and channel it and bring it into your form, according to your level of Love for yourself or fear for yourself, according to your level of receptivity or barrier. It is, indeed, up to you, and when you bring that energy in from Source to the Centre of the Self, and then you say, 'According to the Plan of The Divine, I and All That Is are in alignment. Radiate through me and heal me. I have taken the step of courage to relinquish my control in this situation, and I have said to The Divine, 'It is yours, as it always was, to nurture, to heal, to love as you see fit, no strings attached.'

But for many of you, the no-strings-attached part is the tough one . . .

> No strings attached, I want to be straight in my body. I want to be filled with vitality, with dynamic energy. I want to be thin and sleek and active and intelligent, but whatever it is that I need for my greatest growth and learning, I will accept from The Divine.

And that, indeed, can be a scary process. What if the fear whispers inside you? What if The Divine won't heal you because you don't deserve it? What if The Divine is mad? You took his name in vain. You said to another person, "I hate you." In a past life, seven thousand years ago, you did thus and so. Now you have to pay for it. What if there is no healing for you? Nobody loves you enough. What if there is no God.

It takes great courage to go beyond your ego construct, built up of fears and "shoulds" and other people's opinions. It takes great courage and great strength of character to come to this decision gate and say . . .

> I choose a better way. And because I am in this limited space, this slow place of dense energy, but because I understand and know that miracles do happen, and if for one why not for me—if for that one why not for me—I choose not only to believe in miracles, but because I know belief can be changed, I choose to expect a miracle. I choose to be receptive to that miracle, and I choose to give my Love and Trust to The Divine, knowing that if this condition, circumstance, or environment that I live in, whether it is my physical body or the circumstances around me, if it appears that they remain the same, I still trust that I will be taken care of. It may not be according to what my limited knowledge says, but I trust that I will be taken care of.

And so you have the courage to say, "No strings attached. Heal me according to what is best for me, for You, for us, and for All Life Everywhere," because I remind you that you did not incarnate into a Universe of one individual, that everything you do touches everyone else, and what happens to you, and what choices you make, ripple and pulsate and touch many, many others. Are you going to be courageous enough to lift yourself out of the corner, to take yourself without fear, without shaking, without shame, into the center of that vast space where God, Goddess, All That Is, fills and surrounds you? Are you courageous enough to remember and understand that God only enters into equal partnerships, and when you can say, "I and my God are one," and in that One there are no limits, and when you have the courage to believe that, and the courage to stand up for that, then healing can occur in miraculous ways, and some of that healing will be healing of the Spirit, not necessarily healing of the body.

The Christ in his journey on the Earth plane came on a day of celebration to a small village, and he sent his disciples ahead to go toward the place of celebration. They could hear the music. They knew the dancing and the feasting were going on, and he said, "I will catch up with you," and as he walked slowly and took a turn, he came to a place where a young woman sat. She sat on a cot, and she had a vibration of resentment and unhappiness, and he came up to her, and he said, "Dear Child, why are you not celebrating?"

And she snarled at him and said, "What do I have to celebrate? Everyone is out there dancing. Can't you see these withered legs? I have no reason to celebrate. I can do nothing but sit here. I wish I could be there, but I can't. Go away."

And she turned away from him, and he came closer, and he said, "I'd like to talk with you. I'd like to talk with you about laughter and joy and courage and healing," and as they talked, the Love and the Healing of this Master moved into this individual, and she was healed in the Spirit, and she was healed in the Heart, and she felt a great Joy flow through her, and she felt uplifted, and she knew that Life would always be bright and beautiful and well worth celebrating, every single day there forward, and when the dancing was over and her family and friends came back to where she was to take her to the feasting, they found her very cheerful, very happy, singing her heart out.

And they said to her, "What has happened to you?"

And she said to them, "I have been healed." And they said, "Well wonderful, come on let's go and dance."

She said, "No, my body is as it was, but I have been healed. I was given a gift, and I am so grateful that I had the courage to accept it." And some of them wondered, but many of them understood. She had said, "I will accept healing, no strings attached," and it was a courageous effort on her part, but what an amazing Healing came of that, for her Joy and her beautiful voice, her Laughter, her Love, her great de-Light in sharing her story and sharing songs and stories of the wonders of Life, inspired many others, not only in her village but in many villages around, as they came to hear about this miraculous situation.

If you have the courage to accept what good there can be in your life, no strings attached, you can go well beyond the concept that you have of what can be good for you. Yes, it would have been good for her from some respects to be able to get up and walk and dance and go to the well and fetch water and be a participant in the ordinary village life, but that is the thing. It would have been an ordinary life and over time her healing would have been forgotten.

But because she had the courage to say, "Thy will be done. I accept, no strings attached," there was a greater miracle, and she became an inspiration to many others who, seeing her joy even though she had to be carried everywhere, were able to say to themselves, "If she can be so happy in that condition, I, with my strong body and my capabilities—can be happy too." By accepting the courage of what appeared to be a limitation, she transcended it, the limits of an ordinary life, and set in motion a stream of consciousness and awareness that still has the ability to inspire others thousands of years after her life has ended.

This is the healing power of courage. At the most challenging moment in your life to give over your result through Faith, through Love, and through Trust, using your heart energy, using your courage, you wind up with a result that transcends your circumstances, and each of you has this ability, or you would not have heard this story.

Seek to follow your courage, and it will always come back to you with a bountiful reward. It is a promise.

# The Soul's Courage—Archangel Uriel

Yes, indeed, how delightful if you could see yourselves as we see you. There would be no question as to what to choose, how to inspire yourselves, how to move forward in what direction with what support.

My Loves, this is very much what you are here for. Courage is your foundational energy. Courage is base chakra. It allows you to step forward rather than huddle in the muck and the mire that you have created for yourself, and how do you get out of circumstances that your lack of courage has lead you into you? It is forgiveness, tough Love. If you only knew that forgiveness is for-giving to you. It is a gift. It is a vibration. It is a way of releasing and freeing yourself from those circumstances that would drag you down. It is the way that you let go of your shackles. That is the key, but it takes courage to use it. Have you courage? In bags, if you would only look around and see that.

Do you not understand the courage it took to come back to the Earth plane? Do you not understand the joyfulness, the anticipation, the excitement with which you created your agenda? "After this many lifetimes, I get to check this one off. All I have to do is take a cup full of courage and drink it down, and then, head held high, I step forward."

Wonderful Ones, Radiant Beings of Light, the very fact that you are here demonstrates your courage, demonstrates your passion; demonstrates the enthusiasm that you have brought in here. Courage is red vibration. Your life-blood is red vibration. They are one and the same.

By giving yourself the opportunity to take that step from where you were to where you could be, you are pumping more vitality, more life, more chi, through this physical form. "But I don't want to hurt anyone, and if I say this or if I do this, someone might get hurt." Yes, it is true, someone might.

They might decide that you're hurting their feelings. That is not your responsibility. If you go into a situation with the intention that the occurrence and the result will be for the Highest Good of All Concerned and if you act on that compassionately, then how they respond is their choice. You cannot make anyone feel, do, believe, or have anything that they do not agree to.

When you bring in your courage to step up to a situation and say, "This is wrong, and I will not stand quietly by and agree by my silence," you shake them up, and there are many who need to be shook up. You allow them the opportunity to step outside their rut, to step outside their limited thinking, to take off their blinders and see the wider repercussions of the choices they have made, to understand and know that they are where they are because they have chosen to be.

When you say, "This system, this situation, is unjust," and you point it out, the ripple effect continues until you [or another] says, "I'm taking responsibility for this. Change is upon you. Deal with it, World." When you say, "I am the authority in my life," you are taking on the courage of an adult to move beyond your surrounding, being surrounded by authorities who have their best interests at heart, not necessarily yours.

Even those who are the most compassionate, who hold your hand and say, "There, there, I'll look after it. You don't have to worry about a thing." Sounds wonderful?

Perhaps; but when you say, "Thank you for your support, but I need to learn to do this for myself," you are using your courage, and you are using it in a positive, loving, delightfully responsive manner, so that these individuals will understand that you want to stand on your own two feet.

How would it be if your choice in life were to be a concert pianist, but because someone felt that you in your brilliance shouldn't have to put in hours and hours and hours and hours of practice, so they are going to practice for you—how is that going to benefit you? It cannot.

In the realm of physicality, situations need to be repeated in order that the skill level can be enhanced. It is not so everywhere, but it is so here. We will give you an example of courage: A very famous painter who also loved to play the piano, as he grew very, very old, would wake up in the morning and literally need to be helped out of bed because his body had stiffened up so sternly on itself over the course of the night, and he would totter with two canes to his piano and begin with a small piece where the hands do not have to move far, and then getting caught up in the music, would begin to play, and his arms would move further and further apart and his back would begin to straighten, and he was able, after a few pieces that he was performing, to reach the pedals, and you could literally see this shrunken, shrivelled individual, through the power of the music and through his own courage, grow, bloom, blossom, and fill himself with great vitality.

And then having finished that, he could go and dress himself and feed himself and converse with others and be expressive as he needed to be in his life, but that step from out of bed to the piano, on a daily basis, took enormous courage. It took a Great Love for himself and for the work that he loved to do in order to get to that place where his body could again become supple and free of its limitations.

This is what Courage is.

It is about going beyond your limitations. We have said to you that courage is Martian energy because it is outward moving action. What this Martian energy transcends is the limits of Saturn, and who is Saturn? The Great Teacher; when you take on the lessons of Saturn from the perspective that there is always a benefit when you get the lesson, then life becomes richly rewarding.

It cannot be otherwise. Then boundaries fall down. Opportunities jump up and down in front of you because they know that you have the drive, the determination, the commitment, and the enthusiasm, the desire, the love, for who you can be as well as for who you are, that allows you to go beyond those limits.

We will tell you of great courage: A Soul coming into Life has, as do all Souls, certain items we shall say, put on the Life Agenda. Now this is a Master Soul, and this one has some lessons indeed, but this one also has learned a great many lessons and desires to be of service into the world, and another Soul is brought to him who says, "I wish to try to transcend my abusive past behaviours."

And this Master Soul, in its generosity, says . . .

> I will be there to help you. I will come in after you, and I will give you the opportunity to say, 'I choose the upward path. I choose the path of Love. I choose to do no harm.'

Knowing full well the range of potential that could occur if this individual failed in his attempt, and yet the love of this Soul had the courage to take that risk in order to give this other Soul, desiring growth, desiring to transcend his karma, gave him the opportunity to do exactly that.

[When children come into Life, they are very well connected to the Spirit Realm until approximately the age of three. They are so connected to their Guides and Guardians, to the energies around them, that if they choose to leave and do so before the age of three, there is no karmic payment that is required of them. They have come. They have looked at the situation, then they have said, "I choose to leave this life. It's not going to go the way I want it. I do not see a benefit for myself."

[And The Divine welcomes them back and says, "You are fully loved. There is no fault. There is no flaw. There is no requirement to return in karma."]

This young Soul knew that the outcome of his Life would be changed if this individual, to whom he had agreed to give assistance, failed in that task. This Soul knew repercussions would come forward within the first six months of Life. And if the Soul, in agreement with him, failed as he had done before, that the result for this Master Soul would be a lifetime of consequence, but in his Love and in his generosity, in his coming from the Heart, in his courage, he said, "I will be there for you. I will offer you this gift."

And so the one came in and years later the other one came in, and the weakness of the first Soul, the weakness of the Soul asking for the support, was such that he did give in to the lower vibration, to the abusive behaviour, and the Master Soul bears a disability and a mark that sets him apart from others and will do so for all of his life.

Now the repercussions were very mild because of the courage and the advancement of this Master Soul. It was enough to receive some repercussions but not so much because of the learning, and the Love, and the appreciation, and the determination on the part of this Soul to be of service, that it did not have to bear the full brunt of what could have occurred, and yet there is disability, and there are behaviours that are easily apparent to observers.

Each of you has these types of situations in your life, and it is how you respond to them that determines whether you are tying yourself to that kind of situation or that kind of person, or whether you too will be free because you have the Love and the generosity to say . . .

> I forgive you for not being the person I wanted you to be, you intended to be, we promised each other you would be, and I forgive myself, and I set us both free.

It takes great courage to say words of that nature. It takes great courage to put yourself in situations of risk, but it is how you learn to love; how you demonstrate the Love that wells up within you. Each and every one of you here is an individual who has said, "I will accept the potential of great risk because of the Love that I have for the beauty, the sanctity, and the wondrousness of Life," and some of you have met these circumstances, and they have been traumatic for you; and others of you have met these circumstances, and they have been smoother for you because the partnership worked out well, but nonetheless you did not know, as The Divine knew, what the potentials were, and what the outcome could be.

You had an idea. You had some gauge so that you could say, "No, I don't want any part of that." But you did not know for sure what the result would be, and so you took the risk as did this other Soul. You said . . .

I intend to grow more as a Spirit of Light, as an emanation of Love, and I will do this in a way that allows another to become more than they have ever been.

The Earth plane is a place where you have the opportunity to advance in a spiritual basis far more dynamically, far more rapidly, far more thoroughly, than if you had stayed in the Realm of Spirit. One easily moves through the lessons of Spirit when one is in Spirit. It is a serene place to be. It is a place of growth, but it is gentle, serene, harmonious.

This [Earth plane] is a place of intense, rapid growth if you are willing to work from the standpoint of, "What I do, I do for myself and All Life Everywhere and I choose, moment by moment, to bring forth the energy of The Divine." And so that is what occurs, and that growth is extremely powerful if you follow through on that intention. It moves you forward in a very dynamic manner.

This is where you can progress quickly, but it will not necessarily be serenely and harmoniously. That is not the nature of the space; however, the intention is, through your Love, that this becomes a place where there is that manifestation of support, of encouragement, of communication on a global scale, of humanity finally uniting to understand, not in the head level, but in the heart level that what happens to one happens to all, that any outward moving energy is circular and will absolutely return to its point of origin, and if you send it out, you're getting it back. If you send it out negatively, it will still come back to you fully multiplied, and if you send it positively, lovingly, and encouragingly, it will again come back to you fully multiplied ten times, even a hundred.

But none of this occurs without courage, and as Gabriel has said to you . . .

> Courage is love in action. Courage comes _of_ Divinity, not from, because there is no movement. It is there resident within you. There is no separation. It is in your thought; it is in your heart; it is in your blood; it is in your breath; it is in every pulsation of life—that is you.

When you take a step that takes you outside of your comfort zone, you do so not only on your behalf but on behalf of many others around you. Some of whom you will never know, but you take a step in courage, and it touches many around you, like the advertising for the hair colouring: "And they tell two friends, and they tell two friends, and they tell two friends . . ."

and I will say to you that when you commit an Act of Courage from the standpoint of loving yourself or any other, that vibration circles the globe in less than twenty four hours, and it raises the positive vibration of the entire planet, and it is never lost.

You are the salvation of Humanity on this planet, and we love you for it. We love you anyway, but we love you for this as well. It is another excuse to express our love to you. When you can come to understand that courage is a love vibration, not a fear emanation, then you are fuelled by The Divine and the cost for that never goes up.

Brave Souls, the world depends on individuals such as yourself, and that dependence, that ability to lean on your courage, on your love, on your steadfastness, even for a moment, helps Life to get back on track. In your meditations of Peace wrap it with the Courage to accept that Peace, with the Love to accept that Peace, and you will have an effect that is even more powerful.

We are blessed to know you and to work with you. We applaud your lives. They are significant.

# Courage and Choice—Archangel Michael

Dearly Beloved . . .

Indeed, how very much are we and those who guide and guard you, your other participants in Life, grateful for the courage that has been exhibited as you go through the steps of your life.

It seems that many of you say, "Little me, what impact could I possibly have?" And yet we will say to you that individuals of your quality, of your dedication, of your like-mindedness, have assisted in raising the vibration of the world, the entire global situation, from that energy of mistrust, and dislike, and lack of truthfulness into the realm that is life enhancing and is filled more and more with integrity, and you are part of this transformation.

It has not been something that has occurred in your little spots, all by yourself. It is something that has occurred in the Unity of the Collective Unconscious, but it could not be so if you did not come here with the clear intention to follow that with the heartfelt choices of meeting the obstacles, meeting the lessons, meeting the challenges in your life, in such a way that it could, indeed, manifest, bring into form, share with all of life on the planet.

When we say All Life Everywhere, we are not talking only of the human race; nor are we talking only of this planet. We are talking of the manifestation of life in every form, in every point that it exists.

Have you a power? You come from Power. You were created because of Power. This is a word that is difficult for many of you, but when you em-power yourself, when you put power into your self, your behaviour, your actions, your intention, you are becoming a creature of creativity and manifestation, and like the artist who puts a point, and then a shape, and then a colour on a blank canvas, that takes courage. Like the author who, sitting down to begin to write, puts that first word on the paper or on the screen, you have taken that form of courage to change your existence.

Every thought that proceeds from your mind into your heart, every word that proceeds from your heart and mind into the atmosphere around you, every action that you take, is initiated because you had the Courage to move from a point of stillness, perhaps from a place of fear, into a different future. Every intention you set, every image you focus on, every point that you make a decision, is a point of courage and a point of transformation.

If you were to huddle in the place that you began, allowing yourself to be there immobilized, you would not exist long, but even more importantly you would have been of no benefit, no life-enhancement, no joy, to Life.

And, equally as you are created of Love, equally as you are of The Divine, so too are you of Life. They are, in great essence, the same energy. You cannot have Life if Love is not present. You cannot make a choice from the heart that moves you forward on your journey if Love is not present. You cannot have an impact on yourself or any other if Love is not there.

And you will say, "Michael, what about the person who has an impact on his wife as he knocks her teeth in? Where is the Love there?"

And I will say to you, "The love resides in this woman who takes a great risk and says, 'I give you your choice,'" and know that although in this limited period of Life, it seems like she is getting the bad, the difficult, the raw end of the stick, she is putting herself in a position to transcend that kind of Karma and that kind of situation; so that, she will go on and meet new Karma and new situations and new individuals, and he will meet the same vibration that he has given to her; only, it will be much more intense toward him.

In the situations where there is war, it is a challenging thing for those individuals who believe it is very wrong to take a life, and yet the requirements of their country and their country's obligations, their belief systems, the concept, the idea that they are fighting for or fighting against, puts them in a place that they may not want deep within them, to be.

There are those who will say, "If I'm here, am I creating negative Karma for myself?" Perhaps that is so, and what can they do about it? They can watch their intention. Is their intention to brutally portray life and take it in a traumatic way, or is it their intention to follow their service and do it in such a way that as little harm as possible is done?

Some years ago a very quiet-voiced and calm individual, an actor by the name of Gary Cooper, was part of the recreation of a true story of an individual called Sergeant York who did not believe in killing other people. And yet, because he was not part of a specific religion that held that as their belief, he was required to go into a war zone, to be part of a war situation, to learn how to clean, and carry, and put together, and shoot a rifle with the intention of taking the lives of others. And yet, this individual had the courage and the respect for his life and the lives of others to take that to a different form, a difference state, and wherever possible he wounded or he captured. This one captured many, many individuals rather than simply charging in there and mowing everyone down. It is what he did with the circumstances that he was in that determined the Karmic outcome.

War has been with the human race for a very long time. This recent hiatus from World War II and the end of the Korean War to the present day has been, in essence, the longest "peace-filled" period of time, and even that has had its areas of the world where people have been embroiled in conflict against each other. The Vietnam War was a watershed. It brought to the attention of world leaders that there were individuals who were going to stand up for their principles, for their beliefs and values, and say, "I choose not to participate."

And there were others who would say, "I will follow the dictates of my country." And both of them have value, but the wounds of those who went to war—and were engaged in situations that were not under, what one might call, the Gentleman's Rules of War, the humane engagement practices if you can apply such a term to that—that went into war and through their leaders' dictates, engaged in traumatically, negative situations, that harm not only the enemy but themselves as well . . .

These individuals have been reaping their Karma instantly because many of these individuals were Master Souls who came in to say, "No, I'm not fighting." There was what is called, a bumper sticker in the sixties that said, "What if they gave a war and no one came?" That was part of the intention of the war of Vietnam, and some, with courage, refused to go to the war; and others, with a degree of honour, went to the war.

And those who came back with the stress syndromes and the woundedness of heart and spirit were those who felt compelled to follow orders that made them go far beyond the intention of simply stopping or eliminating the enemy. But the greatest repercussions of those circumstances will lie on those who knowingly ordered the massacres, the uses of chemical weapons that caused a great deal of harm to all concerned. The repercussions of this war will continue for a great period of time, but there are circumstances in the wars that are occurring now that are not as vicious as what occurred in Vietnam because people have said, "This we will not stand for," and their heart emanation is having its influence. The war is still happening; yes, but the influence is shifting the way the war occurs. There are many, many individuals who are still in that vibration.

In part, it is the energy of the previous age of mankind, the Age of Sacrifice and the Age of Victimization that is seeking ways of continuing its existence. Even though Mankind has been in the energy of the New Age of Humanitarianism, of global concern, and the coming together on a global scale for the benefit of All Life in the world so that there will not be this divisiveness.

But this old-age energy fights for its existence and that is why there is still war and still trauma, still drugs and still other situations, that are very devastating to the planet, to the recorders, to the plants, to the animals, to the humans.

Do not give up hope. Extend your courage to those who need it most. Meditate for peace. Do not walk around and say, "I am against the war." That only gives the war energy to fight back at you. Say rather . . .

> I am for Peace, and I choose not to put myself in a circumstance where anything that goes against the emanation of Love and the experience of Peace in my life will be acceptable, which means that if I am at a gathering in my home and two relatives begin to argue, I may excuse myself or I may simply turn and walk away and go to a place where I can be quiet and not have to hear this energy.

It means if there is a program on your television that you have once enjoyed but now find far too harsh, far too antagonistic, far too confrontational, that you will shut it off or change to something else that is more life enhancing, more uplifting, more encouraging, because you choose not to be in that vibration anymore, and this, My Loves, requires great courage because you are saying to those around you . . .

> I am making choices about what is acceptable to me, and I am standing firm on those choices. I would love to have you in my life, but if you insist on being argumentative, of blaming the whole world for your problems and relating those confrontational and vulgar situations that you have had on a daily basis with others, I'm not going to be here because I will not contaminate myself, my environment, internal and external, with this type of energy. I love you dearly, and I choose a life of Peace. You are welcome with me, and I choose to decree and set in place what is acceptable in my presence, and what is not . . .

. . . And there will be some who will be angry with you, and there will be some who will be upset with you or puzzled by you: "You're so different," and then you say, "Thank you, I'm having a blast."

Have you the courage to clearly set your intentions, to say as Wayne Dyer does, "I can choose peace instead of this," and then choose it and follow through on it, or are you going to say, "I really would rather have this, but I don't want to make waves so I will accept what I do not want in order to have peace," and we will remind you, My Loves, that Peace at that price is too costly.

Love yourself enough to draw the line and stick with it. You can do it. You have many who guide you, many who love you, many who encourage you, many who guard you, incarnate and discarnate, who will support your choices.

And you may find that some individuals remove themselves from your Life. Let them go. Bless them and let them go. You will find that their place will be taken by those who have a similar courage and a high, complementary intention to what yours is.

Dear and Wonderful Ones, we love you. Beings of Light, we are grateful for your time, your attention, and above all for your Love. We will gift to you in great abundance, all that you share.[4]

---

[4] See two questions on Courage beginning on Page 217

# CHAPTER VI

# Deserving

Deserving. This is one of the most power-fully dynamic words in the Human language. The sad thing is how frequently this word is used in a negative manner to reinforce the concept of non-deserving.

In these talks, the Archangels spoke from the "Self"-oriented point of view: Self-Worth from the Archangel Gabriel's view; a Self-Healing meditation with the Archangel Raphael; the Archangel Uriel encouraged Self-Empowerment; and the Archangel Michael rounded out the evening with his uplifting word—Self-Value.

# Self-Worth—Archangel Gabriel

Dear and Wonderful Ones . . .

We are here to speak to you about Deserving.

What a tremendous word that is for so many of you. You desire your Life's path, and when you discover how amazingly delightful it is, how much fun it is, how joy-filled and satisfied you are, when it happens to you, you wonder why you deserve it, or if you are worthy of it.

Do you dare? Are you wrong?

Ah, My Loves, Wonderful, Wonderful Hearts, if you could see yourselves as we see you, if you could remember or at the very least trust and have faith that you deserve all the Magnificence,

All the Bounty,

All the Richness,

All the Joy,

All the Delight,

All the Love,

All the Satisfaction that the Most High would give to you, not what you think that you deserve, not what someone else says you deserve or don't deserve, but what the Most High would have you have.

Crystals grow and in their acceptance of what the Divine gives to them they grow into magnificent beings for they are Life indeed.

Plants grow and, without interference, they grow lavishly and abundantly, and they keep growing, and some of them will change form, and some of them will evolve into something else, and they are not the greatest of God's creatures, but they do grow. They do understand the principle of Life which is to go beyond where you are, to become more.

Do they worry about deserving? Not ever.

Animals, without the interference of man, grow and expand. They follow the cycles of Life, and they become more, and when they come to the point of threatening themselves in their environment, they become less, and so the cycle continues.

Do they ever wonder if they deserve the foliage that they find, the other creature that becomes their meal and thus serves Life? Do they wonder when they miss five times at hunting in daylight, "What did I do to deserve this?" They just understand that that is the cycle of Life, and their turn will come.

And then there is Man—the Hu-man, not man alone—apparently the most intelligent—certainly with the potential of being the most prolific predator and interferer with Life everywhere else on the planet that they share with other forms of Life—that they are the ones who say . . .

> What did I do to deserve this? Yes, this is what I want. This is what I am led to believe. This is what I know my Guides and Guardians have been saying to me over and over and over. Am I ready to take it? Well, I don't know if I deserve it.

Do your dreams deserve expression? You have them for a reason. Why would you not express them?

Why would you say, "Oh no, you don't deserve to live. You don't deserve to be part of my Life."

Why not? The dream is God-given.

Deserving, even though this is our topic, is something that you always are. You are deserving of all the positive things in your Life, and yes, Wonderful Ones, because you have chosen them, you are deserving of your difficulties . . .

Not so that you can fall down and say, "Okay, kill me now."

Not so that you can say, "This is my karma. This is my dharma. This is my fate. This is my destiny. I'm just going to roll over and let it run roughshod over me."

Those circumstances that you judge to be negative are there to be transcended,

Are there to be moved past,

Are there to be experienced,

So that you can close the book on them,

So that you can elevate your learning,

So that you can understand the consequences of making this choice, and understanding the entire wholeness of that choice, go on from there and not make that choice again.

Your negative situations, you deserve them as stepping stones to newer, better, brighter.

Sometimes they are deserved to re-balance. They are never deserved to pay back. When an individual has hurt you in another Life, and the two of you are brought together, you will always have the opportunity to hit back, but that is never the Life Plan intention. By the Law of Grace, as we have told you before, Karma can be resolved. Karma can be dissolved. It can be let go of.

And so when you come into that situation again, and you know this person has attempted to hurt you or has actually hurt you, do you deserve this experience?

Yes . . .

So that you can rise above it;

So that you can forgive it; so that you can forgive the other person and forgive yourself; so you can dissolve it with healing, with forgiveness, with love.

But you don't deserve it to be repeated and repeated and repeated, and you don't deserve to be hit with it so that you lie on the floor and give up.

You deserve it so that you can say . . .

> My Life, my choice. I draw the line here. I will never be hit, hurt, or dealt with in this manner ever again because I choose how my Life will play out. I choose where to go from here. I choose to transform this situation and find the silver lining, find the goodness in it.

Because it is always there as surely as the Love of the Divine always radiates toward you without fail, without fluctuation, without ending, without beginning, as sure as that occurs so too is the intention that you bring to you something better, and some of you only will understand through negative situations. It is a great sadness to us, but it is the Truth.

Many of you need to be kicked repeatedly in the leg until finally your leg is knocked out from under you in order that you can finally make the choice and say, "Wait a minute, this kicking is just not enough fun. I don't intend to have it in my Life anymore."

Deserve the beauty in your Life.

Deserve the joy-fullness that can come about when you allow that as a child, a Beloved Child of the Divine, of the Most High, of the Goddess of Your Understanding, of God, Goddess, All That Is,

That you deserve because you were created;

That you deserve because you were loved into existence;

That you deserve because you were given permission to come here;

That you deserve because you just took a breath;

That you deserve because you are about to take another.

You deserve all the Joy, all the Blessings, all the Richness that Life can give to you.

You deserve it all, not just a little crumb. All of it. All of it that you can imagine,

And although we, at times, do indeed mean material things, that is not necessarily a spiritual limitation.

It is an important part because you live in a realm where material existence is what you are doing, but what you are intended to do is to bring a greater spirituality, through the radiance of Love, into this area. You deserve all that Life has to offer, and you have the option and the opportunity of deciding where in the banquet will you put your desires? What part of the banquet would you pick up and say, "I deserve this."

Are you going to pick the dry bread at the beginning, or are you going further down the row and smelling these luscious, freshly-baked, tender biscuits?

Are you going further on and seeing the delight and smelling the aromas and tasting the juiciness and the sweetness of wonderful fruit?

Are you going further on and understanding that when you bless your food, only the goodness that is inherently within it comes to you because that is what you deserve. You deserve all that Life has to offer you.

Your choice is: Are you going to take the good and the bad; are you going to take only the bad; or are you going to take only the good? Free Will is the ultimate rule here.

Of this, we have spoken before, but I say to you, Wonderful Ones, you deserve everything that you expect—and more. There is not one individual in this room, not one individual who will hear my voice [or read my words] that will ever "deserve" only the good because you do not allow it. You do not expect it. You fill yourself with guilt. You judge against yourselves.

You say, "Well, I want to share what I have," and that is a wonderful thing, but when you cut what you have in half, and then you cut it again, and you cut it again until all you have is one little square inch, then you have given away all the other Life-giving essence. That is not what you deserve.

In the Miracle of the five loaves and the two fishes there was enough left over, at the end, that twelve baskets of food were gathered up, and whether you believe that the Christ multiplied the five loaves and the two fishes so that everyone partook only of that and were fully satisfied, or whether you believe that blessing, that high, clear, beautiful, sharing intention touched each and every heart there so that every individual, who had food shared what he had without judgment against those who hadn't thought to bring it doesn't matter.

It doesn't matter how the Miracle happened.

What does matter is that in that moment every individual knew that they deserved a full stomach and great satisfaction. Having taken in the nourishment of Divine energy, the bread to represent the Earth and all things on the Earth, the fish to represent the Christ and the Spiritual Life, but they all knew that they deserved.

And so it was; and it was abundantly so. And that is why the twelve extra baskets: twelve, a manifestation number, a number of creativity, a manner and an energy that brings together separateness and multiplies it.

In this way, do you understand how you deserve as well?

You deserve because you exist.

You deserve because the Divine created you.

You deserve simply because you are.

What do you deserve? Everything you can permit yourself.

Now you will know and understand that, in this permitting, there are many things that need to be overridden or released or dissolved:

All the feelings from all of your Life about poverty,

About lack,

About want,

About "there isn't enough,"

About the sensationalism that you hear from charitable organizations and media and other propagandists that say, "Send to this area of the world. There isn't enough."

Sending to others is not a bad thing. Believing that there isn't enough is the challenge because I say to you, if the food in the world was adequately and equitably distributed, everyone—every single one of six billion plus individuals—would have enough for their needs today.

Be content to understand that there needs to be moral will also looked after. When you seek to know truth, you will discover it.

There is an ample supply for full, very full, little bellies, and their parents do not need to give up what they need to nourish them, for the sake of the child.

So why doesn't it work? Because Deserving is looked on as being negative, as being greedy, as being selfish, as being wrong, by a great many people, and there are others who encourage that point of view.

It is a sadness, My Friends, indeed—that is the way Life is looked at—because it is absolutely untrue. There are individuals who say to their small children as they smack them on the face or on the bottom, "I don't like what you did. You deserved everything you got."

And there are others who will say, "This individual has committed what we have identified as a crime. He deserves his punishment." What he deserves is an opportunity to make recompense, to balance what he has done with equivalent energy. What he deserves is forgiveness, and what he deserves is to understand the depth and the quality of what he has done, the consequences of it, in a very deep manner, not surface, but something that will impact on him, as his behaviour has impacted on another.

We are not saying here "an-eye-for-an-eye." What we are saying here is bring this one in and say to him, "I want to forgive you, but first I need you to understand the depth of the consequences of your behaviour."

Because when one is hit for what one has done, it heals nothing. It mends nothing. It fixes nothing. It only says to the small child who grows up into the adult, that power and strength are the only things that count, that being strong enough and powerful enough to smack others down before they smack you down is what counts, and that has nothing at all to do with the vibration of Love which is the reason why each of you is here.

That has nothing at all to do with Deserving.

No one deserves to be struck or hit down or hit back.

Everyone deserves forgiveness and love, and this is talking about Life.

This is not talking about organizations or bureaucracies that take on a momentum that seems to be almost Life, because often they deserve to be struck down. As soon as they lose their focus on benefiting the Beings for whom they were created—and we are not talking of the owners; we are talking of the individuals, the groups, the creatures of all kinds that they serve—that the moment that service goes out the window, is the moment that organization deserves to be dissolved. That organizations and bureaucracies, philosophies of all kinds, develop the ability to keep going and keep going, and if no one will stand up and say, "I don't deserve this treatment from you," and draw the line, then they will keep going on and on.

When you understand that you deserve only good, only laughter, only Joy, only Love, and when you stand up for that, when you choose it and refuse to lay down, sit down, or jump out of the way so that someone else can have their negative expression of Life, then you can influence not only your Life for the better but the Life of All Life Everywhere for the better. As you stand up for yourself so do you teach others.

The children who are here now know that they deserve a world of Peace, a world of Creativity, a world of bright, loving, positive communication and support. They know this. They don't have to believe in it. They don't have to choose it. That has been done.

This is a knowingness that comes from the Trust in who they are and who they are connected to because they don't forget, and all of you have forgotten. They are here to remind you. They are here to shake you up.

Some of you, by hearing over and over, will learn. Others of you will not learn until you get an impact. Very few impacts are delightful, and so what can we say to you to convince you that you deserve a Life of joy?

Over and over and over we say to you, "Choose happiness." We hold up to you individuals who have chosen happiness, even in your own country, even some of those whom you have already met.

Choosing happiness is the greatest way of indicating to the Divine your choice, your acceptance that you deserve, not only to be happy but to be lavishly happy, not only to feel joy but to feel full of joy. Joy is something that cannot be held down, like the lid on a kettle that must boil itself over. Joy bubbles up, and you deserve it. It is part of who you are. Deserving is one of the most positive and accepting vibrations that you can give back to the Divine with saying, "Yes, thank you, I accept."

Understand, Wonderful Ones, you deserve because you're here.

You deserve because you are loved.

You deserve because you live, and what do you deserve?

More love, more laughter, more joy, more completion, more success, more achievement, more abundance, whatever it is. Life must become more. When you understand that you too are part of this Life that is intended to become more, then you can "get with the program" and accept all that is being offered to you in order to have you fulfill that destiny of Abundant Love.

# Self-Healing—Archangel Raphael

And so it is, Dear Hearts, that we wish to encourage within you the experience of understanding how much you deserve, of realizing that Deserving is part of the Cycle of Creation, the Cycle of Life, the Cycle of Energy flow that goes out, that must come back in, and so it is part of what goes around that thereby has the opportunity to come lavishly around bringing healing in its wake multiplying it.

Dear Hearts, we would invite that you close your eyes and begin to slow your breath that we might bring to you a meditation, a visualization that will facilitate this.

> And so you breathe in the Golden Green Light of the Divine Feminine, letting it fill your body and releasing all that which no longer serves your physical needs . . .
>
> And you breathe in again the Golden Blue Light of Higher Thought, filling your entire space, and as you breathe out you release all thoughts and patterns of thought that no longer serve you . . .
>
> And once again, you breathe in, and you breathe in the Golden Pink Light of Unconditional Love, and it fills all your spaces and all the spaces in between, and as you breathe out every form of condition attached to the word and the experience of Love is released and is fully a part of your self, your Life . . .
>
> Allow yourself to be in a beautiful garden filled with an abundance of flowers and living forms in all colours, in fragrances that soothe and bring you and your vision to a great sense of Inner Peace.
>
> As you sit there, enjoying the view, feeling the Peace, become aware of little cool droplets gently falling into the palms of your hands, into your lap.
>
> How refreshing this is.
>
> How delightful that the strain and stress in your shoulders begins to ease away.

How relaxing that your forehead, your throat, the skin around your eyes and your ears lets go,

Rela-a-a-xes,

Brings you peace . . .

And as you open your inner awareness, you realize these droplets—cool, healing, and refreshing—are droplets of Clear, Golden Light.

They represent the Lovingness of the Divine who created you.

They represent Abundance at all levels.

They show you your ability to receive . . .

You will say to your Self, "This is Magic [for Magic is a word that once meant to receive]. I deserve the joyous Life I would choose from the point of Happiness,"

And as you say this, you notice that more and more drops fall into your hands, fall into your lap.

"I deserve a Life of the Abundant Goodness and Love that the God of My Understanding would shower me with,"

And you notice that the Golden Light falls gently, peacefully, and abundantly onto your shoulders and sticks in your hair. It fills up your lap.

"I deserve all of Life's goodness, for I am loved, and I am good, and I deserve all of Love's goodness no matter how I judge myself,"

And the Magic continues, and the Golden Shower fills you up with its radiant beauty, with its awareness of all that you deserve.

"I deserve peace.

"I deserve success according to my definition.

"I deserve abundance.

"I deserve friendship.

"I deserve compassion and healing, and the opportunity to give these away.

"I deserve contentment.

"I deserve those physical energy rewards manifested according to my greatest desires.

"I deserve the opportunity to be of service that fulfills me as it brings comfort, joy, and upliftment to others.

"I deserve to receive and know Divine Love for no other reason than because I exist."

Give yourselves a moment or two to add to what you deserve, that is positive, fulfilling, and filled with Great Love for you . . .

With an expression of gratitude in your heart allow yourself to come gently, peacefully out of your meditation. Return to the room and, if you choose, open your eyes.

❋ ❋ ❋ ❋

Dear Hearts, whenever you find your energy tightening up, whenever you find yourself questioning your deserve-ability, your ability and your willingness to know and trust that you deserve all that is good in Life, take a moment or two and listen to this meditation again, to bring you back into balance and into alignment with the Energy that wishes Magic to you, that you might receive its delights.

# Self-Empowerment—Archangel Uriel

Glorious Beings of Light: Magnificent, Wonder-full, Loving, Divine—from, of, and through the Divine . . .

How can you say, "I do not deserve?"

How can you allow another authority to hand that to you, and then keep it for your own? It is their fear. It is their teaching. It is yours to choose, as true for you or as their learning.

If you say, "I deserve more than my parents ever have," that is not about rejecting them. It is about empowering yourself. That is what this is all about.

"Oh no, I couldn't." Why not?

Who would be hurt if you understood and accepted and demonstrated the miraculous individual that you can and are to be? There are those of you who will understand that the Christ has said, "Even as I do and more, so shall you do." But if you don't accept that you deserve that ability, how are you going to perform those Miracles.

The world has been waiting over two thousand years for you to accept this, and waiting before that because he is not the first who has come to tell you the Miracle that you are, the Magic that you are, and unless you accept that as a Beloved Child of the Divine, as an individual made of the stuff that the Divine is, that you deserve all honour, all respect, all joy-filled circumstances, experiences, and situations that Life can present to you.

There are some of you, My Loves, who do not even understand that you deserve the courtesy of having someone hold the door for you. It is a sad thing that you are so diminished in self-respect, in self empowerment, that you cannot even allow that.

Every night when you go to sleep and spend time with your Guides and Guardians, with the Angels, with those Beings of Light who love you, they are there, because they love you.

Why do you think they love you? Because God put a stamp on their foreheads and said, "Love this person?" Because God said, "This is my Child, and together we will love this Child."

There is nothing that you need to do to deserve positive things, uplifting experiences, exhilarating situations. Just show up and say, "I accept. I am open to receive. I understand that because the Divine and I are One, I deserve that too."

When you come to the Consciousness of Understanding at the front of your minds, in your ego understanding, in your awake-ness, that all Life is connected, and that; therefore, what any part of that Life expression deserves so too do you deserve it as well, then you will begin to understand.

Deserving is not about who has more money, who was born with a silver spoon in their mouths, who can do this faster, better, et cetera. Even the most traumatized or broken, even the most hateful among you, deserve positive-ness, deserve forgiveness, deserve love.

It is why you are here, to understand that, and when you understand how Magical it is to deserve, then, as you have been told—as Gabriel has said to you: "Magic means to receive"—you will always receive what you tell yourself you deserve [whether you tell others through your actions, whether you tell the Divine in your heart, whether you tell other people in your gossiping or in your pain], what you deserve is what will come to you.

Now, having said that, know that every single one of you has a lot more lined up, waiting for you to say, "I'm ready to receive. I deserve all the abundance, all the blessings, all the Light of the Universe," than you allow yourselves.

Many, many of you when seeing in front of you a beautiful, luscious, tastefully-presented pie, say, "Oh no, I only deserve this little bit." Wonderful Ones, there are days when we would really like to give you the whole pie! You do deserve it. You deserve the richness of it. You deserve the beauty of it. You deserve the flavour of it, because all of that nourishes and enriches all of your Life.

What are you saying to yourself and to others when you say, "Oh no, I don't deserve . . . ?" If someone is offering you something and you say, "Oh no, I don't deserve it," are you saying to them that they, themselves, or their offering is not good enough for you?

Now that may not be your intention, but that may be their interpretation. Think of that.

When a small child comes in from playing with a fistful of five dandelions and says, "Here, I wanted you to have these," what do you do?

Do you say, "Oh, those stinky old weeds, throw them in the garbage?"

What are you doing to that now broken heart?

Or do you take and put them in a little glass and say, "They're lovely. They look so much like the sun. Thank you for loving me because I deserve it."

Many, many, many symbols come so that anything that is in that is as food to you. Many representations of the Energy of Divine Love come to you, and you say, "Oh no, I don't deserve it. Oh no, I can't receive it. Who, little me?"

Who else but you; who else, indeed, but you?

There is so much Love to be given out that when you say, "I don't deserve it," it sets a vibration around you of isolation, of separation, of denying help, denying God. Is that truly your intention?

Some of you say, "I don't deserve, or I am unable to receive," because you do not want to be seen as proud, but we will say to you that this is the opportunity to show—yourself, in particular—how much Love there is in the world because when you receive this, every single one of you knows that it's not going to stop with you.

But we will not say to you this time, "Receive, so you can give to someone else," because when you understand that you are able to deserve, that you deserve to deserve, it is for you: period. For no other reason than because it is you who are here; you that we would shower with Golden Drops of Love, with Golden Drops of Riches, with Golden Drops of Friendship, Companionship, Joy, in all of your Life.

Is it so hard a concept for you to accept, that you deserve this because you exist? I say to you, that of all of God's creations, you are amongst the favourites.

Now, we, as the Angels, understand how much Love there is for you, and we still receive and know and participate in and experience an Amazing Love that can be so difficult to describe in your limited vocabularies that the phrase "you 'kinda' have to be there," is the only one that makes any sense—and it does not even come close.

Love that vibrates through your hair;

That sparkles out of your eyes;

That makes your breath feel like you could encompass the world;

That brings you so close to the edge of tears, and yet you know that that Joy has nothing to do with pain or disturbance of any kind.

It is just so much that the physical self—even extending itself into its auric fields—cannot hold all of it, cannot express the slightest iota of a particle of it, and it is there because it's you, and it is there because it's you, and it is there even for us.

What you have learned about Deserving, very often, can be ascribed to power, to control issues, to that sort of negativity being foisted on the world. And yes, it is true: there are circumstances that are being brought into the world, that you are being told is for your own good but—in Truth—it has your own good nowhere in its intention.

There have been and there continue to be substances put into food to make it more addictive, in a similar manner to substances put into tobacco to increase its addictivity. It makes no sense. People will eat, but there are some power mongers who have decided that they desire you to eat their product, not just a product, and they will add to it or slide under their labelling, to increase the addictive nature of certain foods, and the more processed a food, the more it needs—at the very least—for you to ask a blessing on it so that anything that is in that food that is not for your Highest Good be gently removed from your system and dissolved.

We would recommend that you take care of the liver and kidney systems in order that they can continue their work at detoxifying the body at the most effective levels, and the more natural items you can insist upon or lay your hands on, the better it is for you, and the better it is for those individuals who are highly sensitive: not all of them are the children. Individuals with allergies and asthma, for example, would do well to examine their responses to food because there are agents there that play up that energy.

So many of your corporations are not interested in growing and evolving except, shall we say, sideways, where they acquire more of the same, or they acquire more of other companies, but they are not interested in evolving into something new. They are interested in maintaining and continuing what they already have.

Therefore, you will see so-called health promoting products that assist you in continuing the very situation that you take them to get rid of, and when you know and understand that you deserve a better Life, you become awake to these situations, and you become sensitized to them.

Now we are not saying that you go on the Internet and accept and swallow whole all that you read there. Fifty percent of what is on the Internet is a negative or incorrect or ego self-serving. So use your discernment; if something comes to your attention that doesn't make sense; if something comes to your attention, and you move it slightly inside your vibratory field and your stomach goes "ooup", there is something here to look at further. There is something here that is not good for you.

Many, many, many of the conditions that interfere with the goodness and the brightness and the enjoyment of your lives has to do with what has been altered, changed, or otherwise de-formed, in what you put in your bodies, or what you put on the skin of your bodies or on the hair of your bodies, because those too will take in. We are talking of the scalp area when we are talking of hair. The hair itself will identify what is happening within you, but that is a long and involved process, and when you choose, each and every day, to say, "I deserve the Highest Best. I deserve this food, this product, this drink, this air that I breathe, to be the very best to support this physical vehicle that I have," then you are shifting the energy from victimhood and slavery to self empowerment and attachment to, connection with, the Divine Self within. We encourage you to follow through on that, indeed.

# Self-Value—Archangel Michael

Dearly Beloved . . .

Your patience and your attention in this important topic are very, very much appreciated. You have convinced yourselves that you are power-less, that you do not deserve all that your heart desires.

You have allowed other authorities to make decisions for you. You have said, "I don't want to hear about that. It's too difficult. It's too painful." You have said, "There is nothing that I can do so why should I try?"

We will say to you, Apathy is the greatest enemy you have, and it is the greatest situation that those who are in greed-based mode, those who are controllers, those who are power mongers, count on, that you will say, "I don't deserve this. I'm not powerful enough for this. Nothing I do will make a difference," but My Dear Loves, it is only you who can make a difference.

Always, always, always . . .

Every morning when you get up,

Every day that you sit down in front of a meal,

Every time that you meet a new situation,

Every time you have to choose between this item and this item, remind yourself: "I deserve and I am open to receiving the Highest Best only."

Now some of you will say, "but the Highest Best is always more expensive." Not so.

Sunshine, a trip in the country and a walk in the sunshine, is one of the Highest Best things you can do to soothe and de-stress and heal yourself and it costs pennies in gas, or a two dollar coin on the Metro to take you to the river parks. It does not have to be expensive to receive the Highest Best. As long as you keep saying over and over and over, "I deserve the Highest Best Only," the Universe will hear you and will provide that to you; not to tantalize you and say, "Ha, ha, ha, ha, ha, you can't have it." The Universe is not mean.

The Universe takes you at your own value and gives you that value. If you have a wonderful partner and you say, "I don't know what I did to deserve you," or you say, "You're so good to me. I don't deserve all that you do to me," the Universe will say, 'she doesn't deserve this individual. She has said so. She has claimed it;' then the situation begins to unwind and things fall apart.

You can say . . . I know I deserve you because you're in my Life. I may not know how or why, but I'm grateful, and I certainly am willing to follow my intuition and do more to deserve you more.

In that way, you are expressing your lack of understanding but not in such a way that you are moving that Highest Best away from you. When you say over and over, "I am open to receiving the Highest Best always," the Universe re-organizes your Life so that is exactly what you get.

If you say, "I deserve the Highest Best," you will find that your situation changes—financially, if necessary—to bring you what is the Highest Best energy, circumstance, situation for you because you have claimed it, because you have put yourself in alignment with Divine Energy and said, "I as a Child of the Divine deserve all the Divine would give to me."

Every time you receive a tiny thing or a large thing or an average thing you say, "Thank you very much, God for bringing me what I deserve. I am open to receiving the Highest Best always," and demonstrate that. This is not about breaking. This is about doing your best in any situation, because that too is the Highest Best that you deserve. You deserve the opportunity to do your best, to live your best Life, so that you can continue to enjoy that best for yourself.

You are giving it out, it will come back to you—and if you are finding that the work situation, for example, that you are in is one that grates on you and frustrates you, that constantly brings you headaches or pain or that makes you so full of frustration and pain and sadness to go there, understand that your concept of being willing to accept the Highest Best, deserving better than what you have, is saying to you, "You don't belong here. This isn't the Highest Best."

Then you say, "Well what am I supposed to do? What should I do?"

Some of you who have heard us speak before, will understand that we are about to say: "Let the word 'should' go. It 'should' not be in your vocabulary!"

It is a judgment: you against yourself, you against someone else, someone else judging you. The phrase is, "What *could* I do?" and our answer to you is, "What would you love to do?" because that is the Highest Best for you.

If you want to do something, like race stock cars, and your mother wants you to be a doctor, say, "Mother I love you, and I certainly hope you can come out and cheer me on, but I'm going out to race stock cars." It's not her Life. Maybe she wanted that opportunity for herself and not being able to create it, not being able to deserve it, never got it.

What you need to get for you is what is right for you, always the Highest Best in every situation. Uriel has said to you, "There are many situations that greed-based companies are bringing, that the truth is coming out, and their power to manipulate is being diminished." It keeps coming up.

People diminish their trust in these large corporations because they know that once an individual gets divorced from the person who is at the center of the products' targeting market, the person that they are there to serve—if someone is too far away from that individual—there is no care. There is no connection. There is no apparent responsibility. The responsibility then goes to the shareholders, to the CEO, to the head of the company, to the individuals on the upper half of the employee staff, but to the person? No. All they look at is someone who will continue to buy and continue to buy no matter what. So many things, in many ways, are being adulterated.

For example, there are scratching posts for cats, very useful, piece of cardboard, piece of rope, whatever works well, cats enjoy it, people enjoy it. The pattern is already set. There is no difficulty in having these things be sold on a regular basis. But, 'we want to make it new. We want to make it improved. We want to make the person who already has one buy another one, so we will treat it with catnip.' But catnip, My Loves, for a cat, is a narcotic, and while this cat was having perfectly good use and enjoyment of the scratching post that has no catnip, its entire system is altered by using one that is treated with catnip.

What did it do? What was the intention? The thing worked just fine without the catnip. Was there a real, honest reason for doing this? No. Was there a concern about the home owner or the pet? No.

The concern was to increase sales. They are too far out of touch, like those individuals in the militaries around the world who simply have to push a button but never ever have to look the victim straight in the eye and put themselves at equal risk with their target. They're too far separated from the reality of the situation, and, therefore, are less likely to have concern or consideration, but when you seek the Highest Best, when you know that you deserve Life as you desire it to be, as it brings you joy to experience it, you will understand that this connection, this being involved in your Life, is very, very important.

If you were to simply sit there and open your mouth when someone says to you, 'Take this,' then you deserve what you get, and it may be that what they are giving you is not good for you. It may be that it is good for hundreds of other people but not you.

More and more and more, your health care systems are saying, "Take responsibility for your own health care." This is not necessarily or completely a ploy on their part to reduce their costs. That is one reason; yes, we will grant, that is what many governments or healthcare organizations are seeing as the benefit to them.

But we are saying to you that many, many individuals have said, "We deserve the highest quality of healthcare." So their healthcare system is being adjusted, so that these individuals need to be more awake, more aware, more questioning, seeking more information, not willing to simply allow themselves to be spoon-fed and allow themselves to create according to the word of an authority.

For example, the doctor says to you, "Here's this pill. If you're not better in two weeks, come back and see me," and, of course, what happens? Because this doctor is the authority, in two weeks you're not better, you go back and see him.

But when you take responsibility for your own health, you are then empowered to seek out alternatives, to say to this practitioner of homeopathy or this naturopath or this energy healer, "I believe that what you offer is in my Highest Best interest. I not only believe it, but I trust it, and I know it." Even though at times it feels like the situations that are occurring are negative, there is always a silver lining.

Yes, they are saying check out your healthcare because they don't want the expense, but the fact of the matter is that being more awake and more responsible for your own health care benefits you, because they will be pushed—these governments and these healthcare organizations—pushed into providing preventive services, pushed into providing services that support the body in its most positive state rather than scrambling to fix up a body that has succumbed to man-made illnesses, and so they will.

They will expand because they must, because more and more individuals are saying, "I deserve a healthy body, and your chemical doesn't give it to me."

The pharmaceutical companies will say, "Well we've explored this plant, and we took out this active ingredient. It should work just fine, but there are these 653 side effects." Of course, what they have paid no attention at all to is that all of these apparently passive ingredients are in the plant to protect you from all of those side effects that the single, active ingredient alone could create. The plant is wholistic. The pharmaceutical companies are looking for the one thing that they can say, "I created," so they can copyright it and patent it and gain a great deal more money for it.

Be of good Hope. The more that you understand, know, trust, and practice that you deserve wondrousness in your Life, Miracles and Magic in your Life, fulfillment, happiness, and enormous great Joy in your Life, the world will be transformed to support that. This is not a dream, always.

This is the start of a new way of Life, and it starts by many of you saying . . .

> What I have in my Life is not good enough for me because I deserve the Highest Best always, and I choose it, and I will not contemplate or allow to be spoken to me anything that interferes with that, but I will focus on accepting, receiving, transmitting, sending out, and receiving more of the Highest Best for me. I will make my Life Magic because I am open to receiving all that I deserve.

If someone says that you live in a dream world, and you deserve a kick in the pants to get you into reality, sidestep and say, "I like my reality very well, thank you, because I deserve this kind of joy," and then be on your merry way, and know that, indeed, Life will evolve to support what you deserve.

This can, indeed, be a Life of Magic.

It can, indeed, be a Life that exhilarates you,

That brings a smile to your face,

That makes you want it to be long, lush, lavish, and filled with laughter.

Go for it! Be blessed in all that you do, My Loves, and allow us to pour abundantly to you all that you deserve. That means get a big bucket!

# CHAPTER VII

# Uniqueness

A beautiful gift is Uniqueness—it requires us to follow the quotation from Shakespeare that "above all to thine own self, be true."
Each of us has the Aquarian energy of Uniqueness and distinctiveness within our Life Plan—a place where we are encouraged to allow ourselves

to be different and individualistic. However, there are certain societal beliefs that tend to hold us back, wanting us to be standardized and identical in our thinking and actions.

The Archangel Gabriel reminds you that sameness denies your essential Self; the Archangel Raphael uses a meditation that asks you to remember that living behind walls that are designed to hide or reject your specialness, will not stand.

In focussing on the blessings of distinctiveness and unconventionality, the Archangel Uriel encouraged enhancing radiance as part of your Life practice. The Archangel Michael finished this evening's talks by introducing Choice as the Guiding Force to living your Life in your own perfect way.

# The Box is a Trap—Archangel Gabriel

Dear and Glorious Wonderful Beings of Light, we bid you great welcome.

We are very pleased at this intimate gathering. Know that we are very interested in encouraging you to step outside the boxes that you sometimes tend to build around you—and that is not to say that it is a negative thing to build a box around you,

Because it does give you a sense of stability;

It does give you a sense of security;

It does give you a sense of calmness that you might interpret as permanence even though in the heart of you, you know that All Life flows,

That All Life breathes,

That All Life changes, and that, therefore, it is not in the least permanent.

But it gives you that sense while you gather your forces and integrate your learnings and then allow yourself to move forward according to the next step, the next challenge, the next point of excitement—The only difficulty we have with boxes is when you put the lid on and say, "I'm not even going to peek. I'm not hearing. I'm not seeing. I'm not interested."

Then it is not that you are sheltering or even cocooning or nurturing or integrating, but you are hiding, and that is not what you are here to do. You are here to express the unique part of yourself and, "Yes," as we have said before, "All life is connected; All life is one, but All Life is not identical, and that is the beautiful thing about each of you. You are, indeed, individualized thought patterns, physicalities, emotional states, paths and purposes of spiritual growth. You are all of these according to your own vision for yourself."

There is only one of you, and I will say to you that if you choose not to be the Unique Being that you are, then the orchestra, the Music of The Spheres, the Music of The Universe, that is the creative stream of the Universe, has an emptiness, has a skip in the groove—you might say—has that missing note or tone, and you might not think that your travel through Life is important enough to cause concern, but we will say that without your voice, without your tone, without the musicality, the flow of who you are, the music is nowhere near as beautiful as it is when you allow yourself to express that great joy, that uniqueness, that oneness.

It is, perhaps, for minds that tend to work in a linear fashion, a little convoluted to say that All Life is one and at the same time to say that you, and you, and you are one, even though we have just said that you are all connected together.

It is in valuing the diversity of Life that Life becomes more, and if you will stand back and observe Nature at her finest, not interfered with by what is going on according to man's rules and man's desires, but Nature just filling her spaces by herself, there is great diversity there. There is affluent and lush diversity there.

Your scientists will say, "There are only so many patterns of six-sided forms that snowflakes could incarnate into, and that, therefore, the concept that no two snowflakes are the same is an error," but I say to you, My Loves, it is your science that does not have the vision to know and understand that diversity, that uniqueness, that not being precisely identical to anything else is a major law in the Universe, and so in spite of the six-sided limitation, according to scientific calculations, we say back, anything can be proved with numbers, including both sides of that discussion.

Leaves on the trees, blades of grass, motes of dust, faces, hands, hearts, and many, many, many more are unique to the individuals who bear them. Whale watchers and marine biologists identify different whales according to the notches and the pattern of notches in their tails because each one is unique, according to the experience of that being—so it is with individuals: fingerprints, eye patterns, ear shape—all of these—are unique to one specific individual.

So why would you choose to pattern your Life and become the clone of another individual, even if you do so out of admiration and respect for the Life path that they have chosen? Those who are your greatest teachers tend to run in two ways. Some of them have no idea that they are teaching you, have no concept that years and years later you will think of them as one of the greatest influences in your Life. Indeed, if they were to hear that, it may shock them into a whole new concept about themselves, and that would be excellent because then they would have the understanding of themselves in a unique manner, a new way, an expanded way of looking upon themselves, and so it is a highly beneficial thing.

Other individuals, more consciously aware that they are teaching you, teach you what they know so that you can take it, personalize it, follow the basics, but make it yours. Make it who you are. It is fine—it is to be encouraged—to acknowledge the source of your awareness, but know that as you work with it, you may change a word here; you may change a step there; you may add in something that you have learned from another source and come to trust and feel very good about, but in that way you open into your own potential of being a teacher, of being a guide on the way to Life for others, and that is an excellent thing because as you learn and grow through what you have been taught, so it integrates in you. It does not integrate in she or he who taught you. It integrates in you and develops a resonance, develops a level of integrity within you so that as your flavouring, your personal stamp goes on this information, as you transmit it, it becomes exactly what those who you teach need to hear.

When you teach another something that you have learned from one of your teachers, you are attracting to you individuals who might not have been able to go to this other teacher, whether it is through difference in vibration, difference in personality, location, travel . . . There are a great many reasons why this person, who thinks you are the greatest teacher on the earth, could not have been taught by your teacher: because they needed your personal stamp on whatever it is that you are sharing with them, and if you don't think you're a teacher, let me disabuse you of that "fact." Everyone is in earth-school, as it is sometimes called, to learn, and as they share that learning, to teach, and sometimes as you go over and over what you have learned, what you are prepared to share with others; hopefully, you will learn one more dimension, one more facet, about yourself so that once again you can step toward the Beingness of you, the culture of you, the Oneness of you. There is a great deal that can be accomplished when you share your heart's awareness with others.

Now, it is true that there are places on the earth . . . if someone is to pop up a little bit stronger than the others, be a little bit too different than the others, they can still be knocked down until all learning is at a level field, but that also diminishes creativity. It diminishes seeing solutions that require a different point of view. It diminishes potentiality, not only in problem solving but in developing a new Way of Being, in whatever creative manner that individual could have manifested had they been allowed and encouraged to become their own unique self.

You have heard of instances—children at very young ages, five, six, having their works displayed in art galleries where they bring in hundreds of thousands of dollars for amazingly beautiful and unusually precise, diverse, intense works of art. They are living up to their uniqueness because they have not had the years that you have, of denigrating that ability, but it would not be so safe for them to be here if each of you hadn't said, "I choose to walk this path. I choose to be singular, to be one-of-a-kind, to be different and to be okay with that."

If you had not said, "I will express this part of my life which is so different from anyone else that I know," it would have been more difficult for these children to incarnate because the world has learned from each of you that they [the world] must adapt to you, not the other way around. Technology is part of that if it is properly developed. There are some technologies that are in essence a clone of accounting and business practices that were done by hand centuries ago. They have simply been sped up, theoretically, but the format has not changed, and there is the use of technology in connecting and in creating one-of-a-kind paths, or responses, or workings that suit you or you—yes, there is the capability of that. So when your bank says to you, "Our system does not allow that," say to them, "It should." Say to them, "It is appropriate that it does so because I have this as a necessity, and if you can't provide the service, there are many others who would wish to do so." It is a learning that individuals such as yourselves, in a service industry are coming to understand, that if you don't take care of the customer according to the way the customer has its needs, then someone else will.

Greed-based systems tend to say, "Adapt to us. We have all the cards. We'll deal the game the way we want. You have to live with it." And, there are other companies, and other organizations, and other entrepreneurial developments that say, "You have the need; we believe we can fulfill it. What can we do for you? What do you need from us that will make you feel fulfilled, happy, content, taken care of?" And so, they are responding to the uniqueness of individuals. More, and more, and more that is the way of the world.

Statistically, in this country, the greatest development of businesses is through entrepreneurship, small businesses, one or two people gathering together to say, "This is something I think would work. This is something I think people would desire," and they go from their own unique perspective, and they begin, and they develop it, and for many that creates employment for others; and for some, it is developing their own uniqueness into a service that they themselves are able to provide.

And I will say to you as well: Interesting . . . that there are feminine energies in this room—in this country the greatest growth of business development are those businesses, very, very small or even very large, that are headed up by women. At long last, you are coming into your power, and you are doing it not in the way of saying, "Let's dump all this patriarchy nonsense out of the way so that we, the matriarchs, can take over again," but this time you are saying, "Let us work together. If you think you are going to run my life anymore—now that I have my shoe at your throat!—let's talk. My turn first because your chakra is blocked." And so, this is what is happening. It is becoming an integration, but once again it is the Divine Feminine leading the way.

Part of that comes from the Feminine Energy of Creativity. Every single female who births an idea, a child, a concept, a new pattern of clothing, a new arrangement in a room, every female who births something new into the world, understands the process; understands creativity at a very, very basic level, understands that when they are going through this process to create whatever their end result is, it is individual and unique to that specific end result. Every process that involves a pregnancy—for the birth of a human child is unique—every single experience is different from another, because it is a different Being being created. Every single book written is a birthing that is a different process in some form or another than the ten dozen before and the forty dozen after because they are not cloned energy. This is about following your instinct not only to be different yourself but to bring additional diversity into the world.

How boring would the world be if everyone had the same hair cut, the same colour of hair, drove the same vehicle, painted their houses the same colour, slept on the same beds, ate the same foods, went to this place at this time? How boring, how predictable, how full of emptiness, how empty of Life because diversity which is the end product of uniqueness must involve Life-energy? These same chairs on which most of you are sitting, they are a form. They are a product. They came out of one single, unique idea, but there is no Life energy in them because they are the same, the same, the same, the same, the same, the same.

Diversity relates to Life. Uniqueness is the way in which each individual expresses their diversity. And so, we lay the challenge on the table for you: How will you express your uniqueness next time? Shake up your world! Be a little more different than you were yesterday.

# The Walls are Insecure—Archangel Raphael

My Dear Hearts, indeed, for this evening I would love the opportunity of taking down a layer or two of the walls of protection so that you can see out and see what lies beyond them and discover for yourself, "Is that good enough; is that safe enough; is that beautiful enough, for me to decide to participate in, in my own individual way?"

And at the end of this meditation if you have seen—and you desire to contemplate further—then the walls will go up but in a different manner. We will set up the Walls of Divine Protection so that you can see through and do not have to tear anything down in order to understand what is there waiting to welcome you.

> And so, My Loves, allow yourselves, as you gently breathe in and gently close your eyes, to relax . . .
>
> To let go of your tension . . .
>
> And breathing in again a Healing Green and Blue Light that touches the mind, fills the emotions, heals the physicality . . .
>
> And as you breathe in again empower yourself to speak your truth. Fill the throat and the throat chakra with an amazing Blue Light that then fills all of who you are, your Truth, your individuality, your voice . . .
>
> Breathing in a rich, beautiful, Rose Red and allow it to go to the Seat of Passion, the Root Chakra, filling all of who you are and all of who you would love to dare to be. This is your driving energy, your passion. This is where you gather the courage to go forward with bright red boots and walk, and dance, and skip, and slide along your path, your one and only path . . .
>
> And breathing in again, allow yourself to breathe in a breathtakingly Healing Green Light that goes to the heart of you, that goes to the center of you . . .
>
> And having reached the center of you; be aware that the Golden Love of Divine energy sparkles through this Greenness, and it goes

throughout your entire vibration, balancing and loving, centering, according to what is best for you, then all others . . .

Give yourself the opportunity to breathe in an amazing Coral Light and this goes to the Sacral Chakra. This is the point of individuality. This is the point of uniqueness. This is the point where you step out of alignment with all Life. And in safety, with creativity, for a greater sense of health, this is where you create your Life so that you can experience security, calmness, vibrancy, and enjoyment in all that you do . . .

And now allow yourself to breathe in an amazing Indigo Light, moving it up to the third eye centre, and allowing it to flow into all of the bodies, all of the dimensions, all of the places of awareness. This is your intuition. This is your inner sight. No one else sees like you see. No one else interprets like you interpret. No one else encourages like you do . . .

And take another deep breath and bring in the Brilliance of Yellow, bringing it into the Solar Plexus Chakra, activating all the areas of your mind: Conscious, subconscious, super-conscious, and God-conscious—that you might know Joy in all that you strive for; that you might know clarity, and certainty, and discernment, letting go of doubt, hesitation, and self-criticism . . .

Breathing in an amazing Violet-White Light that rises with the gentleness of rain to the Crown Chakra and then fountains down throughout, within all that you are:

Healed and healing, loved and loving, guided and guiding. This one is for you, whether you choose to be different, whether you choose to be the same, know that it is done in your way. This is where you release intensity. Intensity comes from the Base Chakra. Integration and gentle intention are gifted to all energies, all situations, all experiences in your Life when you work with the Crown Chakra.

See around you the walls that you have built up to make yourself the same as any other, to keep yourself safe, to let you do what you do within the confines of your hidden energy, your cell, your cave, your hiding place.

For as you say, "I choose to look on my Life as something to celebrate and look forward to, in my way," know and understand that the first layer of this protective space you have created dissolves and is replaced by the clarity of Divine White Light, sparkling with all colours but clear to see through, and as you say, "I choose without shame to be the person I would love, respect, honour, and cherish in my individuality, owning my own self," see and be aware of the second layer of this defence dissolving, being replaced again by the iridescent clarity of Loving White Light.

Allow the barriers to come down until you can easily see a path—your path—that lies before you. As you look out at it, all you can see is encouragement, lovingness, and that little twinkle that comes when you do something very special that no one else can do. Will this encourage you?

Allow it to speak to you of your beauty, of your potential, and of the desire and the need of the Universe to have you become the greatest that only you can become. Experience this, and we will call you back . . .

❈ ❈ ❈ ❈

Allow yourself to see, but as you contemplate the steps ahead of you, this clarity, this protection, this loving, beautiful Light extends itself along the path in front of you, to shelter, to guide, to love you through the next steps. It is an invitation and a promise that although you are being yourself and your oneness, that the Oneness of Divinity is always within you, without you, always there to enjoy your individuality along with you.

You are invited to take this step, putting your hand in the hand of All That Is.

The next step is your choice.

With great hearts and loving blessings, allow yourself to return from your meditation.

# The View is Unexpected—Archangel Uriel

Radiance—you are all radiance, and we honour that radiance, indeed. So how are you going to shine your light?

How are you going to express, bring yourself out?

How are you going to be your individuality?

This is what your journey is about. The journey of the Soul is to become One with the Divine, by sharing with the Divine all of your experiences, by bringing forward that unique perspective, each and every one of you.

We will introduce you to an interpretation for the Tarot card called the "Hanging Man." This is not about punishment; this is not about being destroyed or hung out to dry. The Hanging Man looks at Life from a different perspective because he is upside down in the card, often hanging by one leg but not in a way that is Life threatening, often depicted with a halo around his head and a blissful look on his face because he does according to his Higher Guidance, according to his moral outlook, according to his own unique perspective, what he feels is important to do, what he feels drawn to do, what he has chosen to do, and he does it in spite of the opinions, or the questioning, or the uncertainty of others around him.

He does it because it is the right thing to do or the right time to do it. He does it because he can express himself in a quiet way, but in such a way that everyone knows he is being true to the heart of himself.

They may think he's crazy while he's doing it, but obviously he's at Peace with himself. That has to count for something, and so it does. When you follow your heart's desire, and you are at peace with yourself, you are not judging yourself according to anyone else's standards, including the one you were programmed with as a child or coerced into as an adult by the beliefs, the "shouldings", the statements, the influences of others around you, significant or otherwise. He follows the heart of himself. He follows what he believes will be for the Greater Good, according to his perspective, which often means he is looking at Life very differently from the way Life is looking at him.

He says to you, "Being different is okay." Being different can be something that is amazingly wonderful; being your own unique self is like going into the birth process. It gives you a new chance to experience Life according to your Inner Self. It gives you the chance to birth yourself, and as you are going through this gestational process of letting go of what you have been told, letting go of what someone else expects of you, letting go of the Life somebody else wishes they could have led, letting go of this shame and that instruction, so that you can create for yourself a tiny, perfect being—your

Life—and so you can love it, and you can nurture it, and you can cherish it until you are willing to step forward into that Life that you have created, that you are birthing, and you can toddle on your way.

And know that if no one else seems willing to support you that you have your Guides and you have your Angels, and they are closer to you, more concerned for you, more loving of you, than any other incarnated individual—if that needs to be the case.

You are creating yourself as you were intended to be, as you set in your Soul-contract that you would be. You are now living your true, W/Holistic Life, and as our Wonderful Friend, Michael, will say, W/Holistic—please spell it with the "W" and the "H." The "W" for wholeness, for all of who you can be, and the "H" for the holiness, the sacredness, of who you are, the Joy and the Divinity that you are. You do not need to become. You are all that we urge you to be, all that we recommend that you do, all that you have come here to do, is to say:

> Yes, that is who I am. I am one unique learning organism in the vast body of the Divinity, and as I go through my journey and learn my lessons, seek out my Joys, step away from those circumstances that caused me trepidation or despair, as I do all of that, I learn; I love; I laugh; I hurt; I heal; I transcend; I die.
>
> I continue all on behalf of myself, my Soul, my growth, and the Divine's, but it is not a matter of me and the Divine. It is us together. We are one. We are unique. The way I am of the Divine, no one else can be; no one else has had the lineage of experiences; no one else has the genealogy of my understandings; no one else can give to the Divine within me what I can because it is my experience, and together it is our experience.
>
> The Divine within me seeks to know Itself more wholistically, more completely, in a more sacred manner, and It cannot do so unless I make the choices, but It empowers me so I can say, 'This is the only way I can learn or I can do this,' and It will say, 'As you wish,' even at the same time as It is showing me another choice on the menu, and sometimes when I am confused, sometimes when I am faced with many, many choices, sometimes when I know I could step back into the fold that is my family, my country, my partner's family, my society, simply by choosing this and this and this off the menu, I can say, 'Bring me a different menu I'd like to try something new. I am open to change; I am open to beginning again; I am open to being me—the one-and-only-one in the family with red hair.

Therefore, I can also love Indian curries because I'm already different, and even though I look exactly like my grandmother, my mother, my daughter, I can still step out of that lineage and say, 'I choose to be my different self. I choose not to manifest this ongoing strain, this practice of living life with migraine headaches. Yes, my grandmother did it. Yes, my mother did it. Yes, my daughter does it. Yes, my grandsons do it. But I choose to live a different path. I choose to let that go with the hope that as I honour and nurture and love myself in this unique way, that I can assist my daughter, my granddaughter, in changing and at least trying what I share.'

This is self empowerment. This is giving in to you all the courage that you might ever need, and the good news is once you've done it two or three times, it gets an awe-full lot easier. Other people's opinions begin to have less and less influence. They tie you up less tightly. You become free.

Is that scary?

For some people, "Yes, it is." For some people it is very scary, and so they take one little step, and they say, "I will follow this life as I have been trained, and traditionalized, and programmed to do, but on Thursday nights I'm going to do one thing different. I'm not going to go to the movies as the whole rest of the family does. I'm going to go to a séance, but I'm not going to talk about it just yet."

You do it to the level of your comfort plus one step. That is what developing your uniqueness encourages within you. Every single one of you has Aquarian energy at some place, at some point, and the Aquarian energy, in spite of its global perspective, in spite of its humanitarian outlook, wants to do it in a way that is unique, and different, and special to themselves. Every single individual on the planet wants to be special, and that is a good thing. Nature loves diversity, and so you have the Sacred Feminine of the Nature aspect of you, and you have the Divine Masculine as well, urging you, "Live your Life, not your parent's lives, not society's life—your Life."

Perhaps you will do it in a flamboyant way with no fear, or at least no fear that you show, and let it go. Let it be out there, as if you are saying to the world, "I dare you to judge me. I dare you to put me down. This will not happen."

But what we will say to you is that you can also do it in your own unique way. If individuals understand that a red suit on you means you're in power mode, and you've got your power suit on, and they begin to prepare for that, then put on a disguise. Wear some underthings that are red so that they won't know, necessarily, that you're in power, because they can't see it. But then you can take charge, then you can be the directing force in your Life, then you can allow yourself to be creative in any area that you would love to change. Being unique means that if someone says you need this medication, and you're really not happy about taking medication, say, "Let me try it at half strength first," because you are already working on empowering yourself to heal yourself. This is your uniqueness. The minute someone says to you, "Well you should or you have to," instead of antagonizing them by saying, "No, I don't," you simply say to them, "I could."

That educates them. Or, "I choose to do this other instead." Sometimes for some individuals who have the finger shaking in your face and are "shoulding" on you constantly, you need to bring them up short and say to them,

> No.—I appreciate your intentions for me because you feel that you want me to turn out well, but you don't always know what's better for me than I do. So I will take your advice under consideration, and if you see me doing something different, you'll know that I decided to take my advice.

But, to some of them you'll have to say, "No, I don't have to do this," and then they will understand that they are trying to interfere. Being unique does give you the ability to stand up for yourself. Being unique says,

> Take all of the things that you have learned and mix them all altogether until you have a beautiful batter, and then put it in your own cookie mould, and push out cookies according to your shape. Add in a flavouring that is your flavouring, not the flavouring you have been told about before; put in a colour; enhance what you have been given; integrate what you have been given with other things that you have learned; make it your story told in your manner because you are attracting to you the people that need to hear it from you, not from another.

Being unique—it is a challenge; it is a responsibility, but most of all, if you look on it with the Hanging One's point of view, it can be an amazing delight. It can be a great deal of fun. You are walking a path that no one else has explored before. Is that not exciting?

Take a like-minded companion with you if you are afraid of getting stuck, and you don't know how to proceed, and you're not sure you'll be able to backtrack. When you become unique and when you check on, and process, and demonstrate that degree of individuality; then, indeed, you are living Life according to the terms the Divine gave you. Never did the Divine say to you, "Prior to Life or at any time here in Life, you must be identical to . . . You can only be the same as . . . All individuals with your hair colour, in your shoe size, or your address have to be identical."

That is not what you are here for. You are here to become all that *you* can be or that you can be or that you can be. This is like the creation of an amazingly beautiful, luxurious, rich, soft, comforting, patchwork quilt made out of velvets, and silks, and other lush fabrics; and each one has its own unique shape; and each one has its own vibrant colour; and each one has its own special embroidery. And together what an amazing circumstance can be created.

How wonderful would it be if everyone created their own environment according to their Higher Guidance and the needs of their Life circumstances, if one individual created a home that looked like it was sculpted out of a tree in the middle of a forest; and another created a home that had streams of water flowing through the rooms to bring that sense of freshness, and movement, and aliveness; and another individual created a room, a house, that was round, but each segment of it, like the segments of the medicine wheel, had a purpose, had a joy, had a vibration, and all of them together supported Life everywhere, but each of them individually gave that person who needs variety the opportunity to be in motion throughout the circumstances of their Life?

"That would be a challenging thing," you say, and, yes, indeed, we agree, but how many carpenters would be interested in what they are doing because it is not the same thing as they did last year, two years before, and as they are looking forward to doing for the next twenty-five years of their lives? By keeping that level of interest and by being part of a unique creation, they themselves are filled with the energy of unique creativity.

Accidents happen because people are bored, because people hate what they do; because people are hurting as they do that, their attention slips, and there you go, accidents occurring. But, when someone is working with something that is unique and different, that evolves day by day, that fills hearts with grace, and fills your own heart with contentment, that allows you to know that even though you are on this planet temporarily still you are on this planet and are leaving your mark on Life. Rembrandt chose to demonstrate his uniqueness through his paintings, and four hundred and fifty years later in Belgium they are using this entire year to celebrate this unique individual. And if you say, "Well, I'm not looking for hundreds of years of fame," that is fine.

What we are saying is, "This was a Life that was lived according to what fascinated, what passion there was, what creativity there was, what delight and joy there was, according to his rules, his dictates." This is what we are saying. If you want on-going long-term fame, that can be created. If you want to work quietly in your corner, doing whatever it is you love to do, that too can be created but not if you are going to hold yourself inside the blocks, the cell, the cage, the hiding place, that ticky, tacky little box that is the same as every other one down the street.

Start your own personal revolution. If you go somewhere where everyone wears this type of clothing that is fine. Put your unique stamp on it. If you go and work in a bank where everyone wears navy blue and black, come in in your amazing, bright yellow suit. After all, yellow is the colour of joy. You cannot help but uplift the energy there. Yes, you will stand out; yes, you will always be remembered, but you yourself will feel better because you are being true to the heart within. And so long as you work honestly, according to your high standards, it will not matter if you wear sky-blue pink with yellow-green dots. Try a little revolution.

Set, determine, and intend. Ask that this be different than it was, and when you ask the Divine that something be different, that you want to be unique, that you want to be the only one in the city, province, country, or world who experiences this thing in this manner, that's wonder-full. That is amazing. That will be responded to . . .

It only needs to be a little revolution to begin with, and yet, we will say to you, "Revolution—it is the re-evolution of who you are." You have evolved to a certain state. Now you have a choice. Will you be the individual that you say in your heart you are, or will you be a cookie-cutter clone of all others around you? If you decide to be the same as others around you, your evolution must slow down in order to be in harmony with them, but if you want to continue to grow, if you want circumstances in your Life to change, then what is needed for you is to re-evolve, to have a revolution of one that says, "I choose to be happy; I choose to serve others with love; I choose to send that radiance, that lovingness extravagantly into the world, and if you think I'm different because that's what I do, well—we will give you a word for that . . . The word was created by a very special individual—one well known and well loved by the Channel, and the word is "weird-a-ful." It is the combination of "weird" and "wonderful" and when you put them together and laugh at the idea and accept that that can be something fun for you to do, then, My Loves, then, Wonderful Ones, then you are on the way to being your truly unique selves, and every unique Angel and Guide who is with you celebrates. Your uniqueness can be used to create that which you love. Choose well. Choose frequently. Choose and laugh . . .

# I AM Choice—Archangel Michael

Dearly Beloved—

Why would you want to be different; of what value is it? How does it serve you?

It is so much easier if you can go along with the crowd. It is so much easier if you don't make waves . . . Or is it?

It is a choice. It is your ability to respect, and respond to, and nurture the part of you that says, "I am special," the part of you that says, "I deserve," the part of you that identifies, "I AM." If you cannot identify with the I AM that you are, then you are not unique. You are not individual. You are as integrated, as de-individualized, as if you were Borg, and you say, "We are."

Now, yes, there are empaths who say, "We are," because they sense themselves and others, but they still have the capacity; they still have the understanding; they still have the ability, to say, "I AM. I choose; I feel; I understand; I experience; I decide."

There would be no word for an individual if that concept was outside of your thinking, outside of your abilities, outside of who you were intended to be. And so, for the very reason that your language says "I"—different from, separate from—maybe strongly connected to, through family, through heart, through race, through creed—but still "I", the one and only me, I AM who I choose to be, or I AM who I choose to allow you to tell me to be. But nonetheless, because you can understand that, because you can conceive of that, that is your basic awareness—that, indeed, you are unique. It is inherent within you.

If you choose to be part of a culture where everyone wears the same clothes, and everyone performs the same practice, and everyone sits in the same chairs, that is your choice, but nonetheless, within the heart of you, you are still your own being, your own self. Some of you will be always, in spite of how much you try to be the same as . . . There will still be differences. Even with identical twins there are differences. One might have a mole just below the eyelash on one side of the face. The other identical twin might have no mole or a mole on the other side of the face. They are still unique.

And so, what difference does it make if they are unique, or if you are unique, or if they are the same, or you are the same? Why would you want to be unique? Of what benefit is it to you to be unique? Why would the Divine create this diversity, this vast number of uniquenesses?

The Divine creates this because It Itself is One—All That Is, that means One—and so It creates a vast array of Onenesses in order that these

Ones who come of Him, who come of Her—(the Channel does not have a comfort with saying "It" and we would agree because there is more of a diversity of energy within that Being than the language you use interprets as feminine or masculine, than as the neutrality of It)—there is too much passion in this Being for the designation to be It, and so we will say, "the She-ness that is the Divine, the He-ness that is the Divine," desires to know Themselves better, and so—each of you, in your diversity, was created so that each of you could experience, could know, could grow, could learn, could share, could teach that Divinity more about Themselves. Your brain, or your heart, the mind, the I AM—and you notice . . . When individuals say or you say, "Point to yourself," they do not point to their brain. They point to their heart.

The heart of your Self cannot physically experience what a hot stove feels like, and so, it creates an extension of Self to touch the stove or to work with the knobs on the stove in order to create heat. But, the heart of the Self has the experience which would not be possible without the individual expressions, and so, you are on a mission. You are on a mission to share with the Divinity all the experiences It has for Itself, for Themselves, and, therefore, for you. When you understand and accept that there is value in being different, when you can dare to be different—and understand the excitement of it rather than the shame of it—then you are truly free, to grow, to develop, to love, to serve, according to your understanding.

When individuals say, "I work with this company, and we have a dress code, and I choose to follow that dress code because I choose to be with that company," they are giving away a part of their essential destiny, their essential dignity, their essential identity, by saying, "I am not worthy enough as I am; therefore, I will disguise myself as this other." And some individuals understand and know that for a period of time that may be the most effective thing for them, but they have another part of their Life where they can be different.

Many, many individuals—especially those on the spiritual path, understand or feel as if they are living Life in two different boxes, and one is their spiritual Life, and the other is their ordinary, everyday, mundane, put-food-on-the-table life. They never feel that they can integrate the two, and so part of them may live under someone else's power, someone else's dictate, according to someone else's vision, and the other part, they let themselves be free to be in the world according to their vision. And, that can continue for a period of time for some individuals of great stamina, great willpower, or great stubbornness; that can continue for a considerable period of time, but sooner or later these parallel lives need to cross-over, need to integrate, need to align themselves, within the individual. Sooner or later some of the spirituality tends to creep its way into the ordinary every day.

It might be with a book with an odd title . . . But, there can't be too much harm in that? Some of it might be a little bit more blatant—that I'm different—according to levels of courage, according to comfort zones, where you push yourself outside the comfort zone. But, try as you might, I will say to you that you cannot live these parallel lives, these parallel streams, on an on-going, forever basis. Sooner or later, one of them will move into the other and begin to establish its presence there.

Are you going to allow yourself the opportunity to be driving the ordinary, other-directed life from your own direction, or are you going to allow yourself to be swallowed up by the expectations, the dictates, of other people? This is what it comes down to: Whose Life is it, anyway?

And when you discover that it is your Life, intended for your enjoyment, intended for your advancement, intended for your power to create—and that unlike the paralyzed individual who wanted to die and publicized their story through the play *Whose Life Is It Anyway?*—you have the power to say, "My Life, and I'll do it my way, and you can't stop me because I am not under your control." What would you do if you could do, or be, or have anything that you desire, according to that kernel of difference and uniqueness? What would you create? What would you try on? What would you practice—that made you feel good?

And, whether or not you feel good because you stood up for yourself, you satisfied your urges; you satisfied your guidance, and you did it your way. Or, if you simply said, "I've changed this; I've added this one unique thing. Everybody else wears this item with this colour, with this pattern, but I have a red handkerchief. Everybody else's is white."

If you do it because you want to see if you can get away with it—and that kind of, almost naughty delight, so long as no other is hurt—do it. If it was fun the first time, try it again. If it was a little bit . . . feeling like you got your hand in the cookie jar; you got the cookie; you got away. You're safe . . . adrenaline rush to be that different—if it is an adrenaline rush the first few times that you are different, that you step outside, that you violate someone else's expectations of you, in order that you can be more true, more honest, about yourself—do it.

Did it feel exciting? Do you want to try it again? How satisfied, how powerful, how much fun was it? Can you be more honest with yourself next time?

Because, as you become more, and more, and more honest with yourself, you feel greater and greater sense of peace, greater and greater sense of satisfaction, and that radiance, emanating from you, gives you the opportunity to say to another, vibratorily, verbally, however it is that you do it, "You too are unique and wonderful, and it is important that you sing your song, that you create your difference, that you march to your own drummer, that you experience the joy of being w/holistic—who you are."

It is an important thing indeed—that you understand the tendency of the world to want everyone the same. It's for convenience. It lumps everyone into the same mould, and if everyone is in the same mould, then you don't have to make this size or this accommodation or become a specialist in this other thing because there's only four circumstances in Life. When individuals decide and honour their uniqueness, they empower themselves to say to someone, "This is not appropriate; it does not suit me, and I am the representative of many thousands of others who have not yet learned to use their voice—Try something different."

When you stand up to an organization or a situation that would bully you into doing it their way, simply because it is more convenient for them, not necessarily that it is more effective, for either of you, but they don't have to think as much; they don't have to accommodate . . . when you say to them,

> What you are doing is inappropriate. I value myself enough to say, 'This is not appropriate for me. I am giving you an opportunity to grow in service, by accommodating me, and understand that my being accommodated will draw to you others who need a similar form of accommodation, not the same as, but the willingness.'

When you insist that what is right for you deserves to be honoured, deserves to be valued, deserves to be responded to, with respect, with courtesy, and with encouragement—you are sending that vibration, solidly, clearly, into the Universe. You are saying,

> I'm willing to adapt, but I'm not willing to be bullied. I am not willing to give up, and I am not willing to lie down and let you walk on me. This is as far as I can accommodate you and still be comfortable in myself. If you cannot meet me here, then you must know, someone else will.

This is part of the shift from greed-based systems to love-based systems, and when you can love yourself as a perfect, honourable, loving, vibrational representation of the Divine, entitled to honour and respect, and encouragement and opportunity of that quality, then the Universe must respond to you, and those who say, "I'm sorry but if you can't do it our way, you'll have to go somewhere else," will soon find that they do have to go somewhere else, because those systems are heading for breakdown, and it is people who value themselves who are sending them there. If you value yourself, then your tendency is to love and nurture and be part of an uplifting evolution that is part of the changing vibration that is occurring on the earth plane and in this galaxy at this point in time.

There are individuals talking frequently of Ascension. Part of the energy of Ascension is transcending the attitudes prevalent in society today. It is, as Uriel has told you, a re-evolution. When you were born, your mother held you and told you how beautiful and how perfect you were, how wonderful you were. Take yourselves back to that. Remind yourself of that. Remind yourself that your mother was speaking from her heart and the heart of your angels, yours and hers, and from the heart of the Divine as well. Wonderful Beings create wonderful circumstances for the world. Loving Beings radiate love, and Unique Individuals set the stage for personal self-value, for the courage to be who you would love to be. It is an opening-door energy, and so we invite you to open the door to your new Life and the world's evolving Life by honouring your individuality.

It is a worthy trek and can, at the very least, be an interesting and stimulating trip. My Loves, each of you we cherish for much that you are, and much that you are not, and much that you can be, but, above all, we cherish each of you because there is no other like you. Be blessed in all that you do—uniquely.

# CHAPTER VIII

# Exploration

In the final chapter of the Four Archangels' series, a rather unexpected topic was chosen by the Archangel Michael.

Exploration is a way of looking at Life's purpose. To explore why you are on this plane is to be engaged in several journeys that can lead you to develop and grow in many ways that celebrate various, integrated spiritual paths. Exploration facilitates the Archangel Gabriel's Journey of Inspiration; the Archangel Raphael's Journey of Intuition; the Archangel Uriel's Journey of Consultation and, finally, the Search for Peace lead by the Archangel Michael.

# The Journey of Inspiration—Archangel Gabriel

Dear and Wonderful, Glorious Beings of Light have you remembered that about yourselves yet? Are you willing to explore the magnificence that you are; the glory that you are; the beauty that you are? Are you willing to go beyond where you have ever been before in understanding self, in understanding Life's journey? This is an opportunity to look not only beyond the future you have often imagined or wondered about for yourself, but to look into a new future, a future that you and All Life Everywhere are in process of creating because you have been making changes, because there have been energy shifts, because indeed there is a positiveness. There is an ebb; there is a flow that is much more dynamic, much more desiring you to hear what can Life be like. Where can we go from this? Do we have to create the future we are afraid of because we see no way out?

So the energy around you indeed is explore your options; explore what you would love to have happen; explore what you are afraid of having happen; explore compromise; explore releasing, so that none of that that you would fear, or be worried about, or be angry and frustrated about needs to occur in your life. This is opportunity energy. This is coming to understand what your philosophy is, what your belief and value system is, what have you chosen to believe is right and true for you, and what are you going to do about it because, your beliefs, My Friends, your beliefs are subject to change. They are how you evaluate a certain situation at a certain point in time. They are always subject to change. So when you believe something, it is the first stage, but it is not the whole story by any means. When you believe that the world is headed to all-out war, what happens there? When you believe that, you are on the bandwagon, tearing down the road to create exactly that.

That is not exploration. That is being a follower, and a follower who hasn't even thought or considered,

> Is this what I want? Is this going to make me feel like I'm a creator? Is this going to make me feel good about self, or am I just following the hoorah that's in front of me? Am I following someone else who stands himself up and says, 'I'm an authority because I have this advice, or this degree, or this understanding, or this opinion that I have decided is right and true for all situations.'

Is that what you are going to follow?

This time of exploration is a time where you can look at your life and say, "Okay, check that off. That was good. Check that off. I didn't realize I'd gotten it, but there I go . . . check, check, check, check. Oh, here's one. Don't seem to be making much progress on it. Do I still want it in my life? Yes, no, maybe so . . ." And so, you decide. Are you going to toss it out, or are you going to say, "Okay, it is important to my life, and I will put energy into it."

Because I say to you, My Loves, that an image or a moon energy list or any other point of energetic focus without an action plan can remain as a fantasy until you decide to put something into action, some effort, some energy, into the situation to help that change flush out the old and bring you to the new. That is what we are talking about here. That indeed is what is important here.

What do you believe? What do you feel about your beliefs? Who gave you that belief? Is it your belief? Did you inherit it? Does it come up from what you are told is your genetic flow? Is it your parents', and your grandparents', and et cetera, et cetera, understanding? Did some authority, physician, teacher, strongly passionate other individual, say to you that this is the way it is? And so, almost like being hostage to their passion and their authority in your Life, you agreed, but now you are at a stage where you are the authority in your Life. Do you still agree?

Does Life have to be tough? Does Life have to be frightening? Does Life have to be the kind of life where wrongs are the natural order of things, and what is morally just, fair, appropriate? Is that a battle that needs to be fought for? And if so, now that you've discovered whether or not you love your beliefs, they support your self, your understanding, your next step in growth, or not, then you are at the point where you can say,

> "You know I believed this all my life, and now that I look clearly at it, I don't like it. It doesn't feel right to me. You know, when I look at what I believe in, how I feel about my Life and myself, and I look at this, I don't see a match. And yet my mother, my authority, always said, 'This is how life is.'"

And for some of you, that will be a great struggle, to go against, especially those individuals that you love or those individuals for whom there is intense energy between you, to go against that, to set yourself up as an authority who knows better for you than someone else.

That can indeed be a journey, but it is the journey, the exploration, the inner to outwardly expressed travel, that you have come here to deal with so that you can be more clear about who you are. And not only that but about who you want to evolve into, much as some of you would prefer. Life does change. There is no stability. There is no security in the outer world.

Where does security live? Within you. How do you know this? By examining your beliefs and your values, by examining your personal philosophy and saying, "This is important. This is important. I'm not sure about this one. We'll put it over here to give it time to state its case. This one, absolutely not," and away it goes, but when you take that belief that you have chosen no longer to believe in and tossed it away, what happens with that vacuum?

That is the critical point. Are you going to put a new belief in its place? Are you simply going to put a golden white static light there so that that old belief can't creep back in and slide into its place while you're off doing other things like enjoying your life, until such time as you come into a situation again, and guess what pops up? That belief that you have moved out of your Life; it is important.

Understand that energy is never lost, that energy moves, that energy, which is all of Life, communicates. When you take this belief and hold it up and say, "You don't fit me any more," you release it. Say, "Thank you for bringing me to this place. Thank you for helping me understand how I've changed. Now off you go, and find someone else to help. We're done; close-door; thank you."

Because if there is not an acknowledgment that that belief has been released, and that you have put something wonder-full and different in its place, it will seek you out and say to you, "We're not finished yet. I had something to tell you, to show you, to remind you of, to inspire you for, and you just said, 'Out you go. I don't believe you.' We need to have a talk or a confrontation. What do you wish?"

When you explore the inner basis for the way you are in your Life, for the way your Life is playing out, you are empowering yourself. You are saying to yourself, "There's all of this unexplored territory in my heart and in my consciousness, and it's going about its business . . . busy, busy, busy, busy, keep going." It is like looking down at the forests of Brazil. You know that there is Life there, but you cannot see what is happening beneath, beneath the surface . . . busy, busy, busy, busy, busy.

When you leave your beliefs unattended, it is the same sort of thing, and some of them do healing work for you, and you don't know it, and that's quite fine, and some of them are cannibalistic, and they will try to knock down the parts of yourself that could heal yourself in a nanosecond if you chose to believe that, and to say, "I can, and I shall, with ease and grace, manifest that," but these beliefs that are antagonistic to your healing beliefs, for example, will try to hunt them down, will try to undermine them, will try to stomp on them, so that when you need instantaneous healing, these negative beliefs will say, "Well, we're sitting on this instantaneous healing because we don't believe in it, and you didn't clear us from your space." And that is why you need to explore within. That is the first step.

It is your thoughts. It is your beliefs. It is your understanding, handed to you on a plate. These things generally have come to you not because you chose them but because they were the garbage, the passion, the understanding of other individuals around you, and when you realize the depth and range and quality of change that has been in place since the time you were born until this point, you can understand how those beliefs, good though they were at that time, have no relevance here, have little relevance here. They just don't relate. They don't resonate, and that is why you need to take a look at all of your beliefs and say, "Hmm, Golden Rule, great belief, I'll keep this one. Hmm, hit back, take revenge, not the greatest belief, I'll put that in the Out Basket." So this is what is being called on.

You are given an opportunity to shift from where you have been, where your parents, and grandparents, and great-grandparents, et cetera, et cetera, et cetera have been, into something new. This is the opening of what has been called by many names: The Age of Aquarius is one that strongly comes to mind, the Ascension, the Rapture, the Sixth Energy planetarily, the Fourth Dimension, or the Fifth Dimension. All of these are levels of understanding, ways of communicating with one another to describe the intention, and the intensity, and the signature of the shifting energies that have been coming onto the planet. When you explore your past and your deep Inner Self, you are clearing out the clutter so you have room for this newer, different energy, and I only say different. I do not necessarily say better.

What you do with it will determine whether or not it is better, indeed. During this time and as Life moves inexorably and clearly toward the, shall we say, target date of December 21, 2012, apprehension arises, and it is not necessary. Even those beings who find change difficult have had years of opportunity to come into some form of comfort with the fact that change is here. It is upon you. Now then, what are you going to see in 2012? Are you going to see massive earth changes, life falling apart, the loss of all your resources? Know and understand that although certain information is being passed forward on the Internet, and television, and radio, that say, "Be prepared. Make sure you have enough supply to keep you going for seventy-two hours." It may feel like scare tactics. It may feel like it is a negative thing. It may feel like these companies who are saying, "Do this," no longer have the confidence that they will be able to provide food, electricity, warmth, et cetera, without significant interruption.

And you know that that is so because there are places even in this stable country, there are places where people have been without power for days and even weeks, and some of these companies are coming to appreciate their powerlessness under certain extreme situations. These are the people who are responsible enough to their customers and to their own integrity that they say, "Be prepared. Our hope, our intention, is that you never have to use this, but be prepared." It is like, shall we say, storing away the summer clothes. It is not about fear. It is about preparation. Summer will come again and having at least a few clothes until you can explore the shops, that gives you the coverage, and so this is the same thing.

They are understanding that Earth is making changes. They are understanding that Gaia is no longer passive. She is stepping into her power, and anyone who doesn't love her will be hearing from her, indeed, and Gaia wants to greet every life form on her with a great deal of love, with support, with stability. She will no longer sit quietly and feel the draining of her Life energies, not for her sake. She knows she is immortal, and if she were to be destroyed tomorrow, there would, in the bright timing of the Creator, in the instant of an eye, she would be re-created because there is still a bright and wonderful purpose for this Great Being. And so, back to exploring, back to making sure that when you go on this journey, you have all you need to carry it through. This is about being practical.

This is about being filled with integrity. This is about understanding what is important for you because I say to you that what resonates with you, resonates very powerfully because you are in sync; you are in alignment. You are resonating harmoniously with many, many, many others; some of whom cannot speak for themselves. Some of whom are putting their lives at risk to speak for themselves, but you in your quiet way, exploring on your own, and coming to understanding, and coming to resolution, and putting into place a greater depth of understanding, a greater degree of compassion and passion; you, indeed, are changing the world because you lift up and assist other people to accepting that the party line, or the propaganda line, or the fear-mongering that is going on is not necessarily the Truth.

And so, whether it is covertly or overtly, your little intention—sitting in your own room; investigating your own part—inspires others to sit in the privacy of their darkened room, in their thoughts that they do not even dare to whisper to others, and say, "I feel there is a better way. I'm sure there is a better way. I no longer accept what this authority will say to me until I check it out, to understand, 'Is there a better way?'" Each and every one of you, all of those hearing our words, there is a better way. There is a new way of looking at your Life and exploring it, but it starts with the thoughts within because that is where all creation starts.

It will not manifest simply because you have the thought. There is this process . . . but it starts first with what you think of your Life, and what you are willing to let go of in your Life; so that your Life can become a journey of excitement, a travelogue, indeed. And as you explore, in-depth, with excitement, with enthusiasm, you discover that you are teaching yourself. You are moving into higher education. And because you are accepting higher education, more integrity, more moral correctness, more righteousness, which is the right use of energy—it is not a superior attitude—as you do all of these, you are creating a new world.

You are accepting the energy of shift, advancement, education, and extended empowerment, as the first seeds of creating your new world. The thought is like a casing. It is a guidance system for your emotion, but the thought itself goes nowhere. And so, explore. Take a look. Sit yourself down with this emotional belief and this logical belief and have them say, "Okay each of you, explain to me why I should keep you. Talk to each other. Talk to me. No fighting, but explain to me why you are important in my Life and deserve to remain with me, and why you are important in my Life and deserve to be part of my Life. Explain it to me." And whether you do this exploration and this conversation through meditation, through contemplation, through imagination, through journaling, does not matter.

What matters is that you are open to exploring and not simply, like a tiny baby, opening your mouth whenever anyone wants to stick pablum in there. This is where you get to choose what's important in your Life. This is where you can say, "This is good. This is less than good. I would never choose that for myself. I will make so what I choose."

# The Journey of Intuition—Archangel Raphael

How encouraging, this next part of the exploration of your Life—we suggest—is the intuitional exploration. By understanding that the Earth herself, and therefore, all the vibrations that are coming to the solar system, the planet, and All of Life on the planet are traveling into a new form of vibration; this is intended to bring forward a new way of exploring communication, of exploring next-steps, of exploring what is the energy within, that is within the heart, that is within the healing center, that is the emotional state.

For I say to you, that if you are calm, cool, and collected about your situation, it will sit there, hovering, waiting to be inspired, waiting to be shot as from a cannon, waiting for your prayer, your statement, your involvement. What you have sought, as Gabriel has said, is the guidance system, but the heart of the matter, the heart of the driving system, that allows you to follow that guidance system and move through your Life, through your intentions, through your shiftings, all of this occurs with your passion, with your prayer, with your emotion, with your excitement, with those energies that drive you and take you beyond the ordinary.

They can also be driven and inspired and moved by great energy that is highly negative, by hatred, by those energies that say, "Nothing will ever change;" by those energies that say, "I've been hurt. Where's the one who did it. They will pay;" by those energies that say, "My family, myself, against the world." This is where we invite you to bring in the ability of intuition, and, "How," you say, "can my intuition tell me if this war in Iraq or this politician's statements—because he wants my vote, or this bully down the street—how is my intuition going to tell me how to handle this?"

My heart says, "I want peace in the whole world."

My heart says, "I want to be able to trust a man at his word, not wonder what his hidden agenda is."

My heart says, "I want to be able to take that bully before he becomes a bully and love him out of that path.

"These situations stand in front of me right now. How will my intuition absolve me of them? How will my passion, my excitement about things being true, and loving, and Life-enhancing—how will that desire bring any kind of change?"

Your intuition is an energy that goes beyond simply feeling what will occur in a certain circumstance. It goes beyond feeling or intuitively being aware of what is happening with a specific individual with whom you have great rapport. Those are baby steps for intuition. Intuition is an interactive—to you and from you—point of communication with your High Self, with the Divine, with God Energy, Goddess Energy, with All That Is, because you and All That Is are one. You do not have to go through exercises and practice and et cetera, et cetera, et cetera to intuitively know what the Divine would have you do. All you need to do is quiet yourself and say, "Here I am," and then you will know. You will hear the message.

You may find that you are making a turn that you hadn't anticipated. You may find that phrasing from a song keeps going through your head, and going through your head, and going . . . until you finally say, "Okay, okay, I know this has meaning for me. I know this is a message. Some of it's clear. Some of it isn't."

When you have intuition at the level that the shifted energy is offering it to you, it becomes more reliable than your logical mind which, indeed, does not always work well either. And when you understand, and when you agree—body, heart, and Soul—that you will open up that energy of communication, that you will consider and attempt, that you will follow anything that you hear or feel that says to you, "Love would like this," that is using your intuition. We have said, Your intuition is interactive. It is like two who spend a great deal of time inside their auric fields—each other's auric fields—and who have a passion for each other and develop, because of their closeness, because of their love, and because of their belief—changed perhaps, but nonetheless—because of their knowing which takes you beyond belief—so that they have the awareness, that your intuition is a nonverbal communication.

Sometimes, in order for you to be able to work with and process it, it will send you a verbal message, but that message is not the whole story. It is 'how do you feel?' when you hear this. What is your response on a body level when this is brought to your attention? Where would you choose to take this? And as you explore the greater understanding that this energy can bring to you, you will find that this energy began in love. And when you accept it untainted—not unquestioned but without certain beliefs, certain tendencies attached to it—when you accept it untainted by values that make enemies out of anything that is different, then you are hearing the message, not with your ears, not with your eyes, but with your heart and with your High Self understanding, with your Soul-aware awakening and understanding.

Your intuition is the first door into this connectedness, this loving, bright vibration filtered through your Soul, enhanced by the energies available now that have never been available here on this specific earth. These energies want to hear from you. These energies want you to say, "This has been my experience, and I am releasing myself from the continuation of this experience." What's going to fill this empty space?

You are saying to your Soul, "Forgive me my non-belief and let me be healed. Let me be in communication anyway," and that is what occurs, but when you ask by putting a coin on a glass table, you don't have to keep dumping more, and more, and more payments.

You don't have to keep asking, asking, asking. With this intuitional energy, with this expansiveness, it will come to the point where asking is going to interfere with the answer because the answer is already there, and that doesn't mean that you don't ask. It just means that the time between asking and answering becomes very short. With this form of telepathy or intuition, what you would ask is already known, and the answer is already there.

This is where you move into the understanding that past, present, and future are labels applied in order for humankind to understand what is going on. It is like using a big fat pencil, in large size, two-lines-high printing, to teach a small child how to form lines of communication. That is what you have had. Now you are moving into the grace, and the symmetry, and the beauty of cursive writing. This is the flow. This is the exploration of symmetry, of timelessness, of being in a place and a space where your choices are already available in front of you, where what you would desire is already known and stands there, waiting for you to accept it, to receive it.

The energy that is being brought here is not so slow and dense as it once was unless you hold in place a belief that says, "It always has taken this amount of time; therefore, it always must take this amount of time." When you understand that as you stand in the present moment, all of your past is present, active, and beside you, and all of your future—every single choice, every single result of choice—is present, active, and living beside you. All you need to do is stand at the choice point, the now time, and decide: What are you going to bring in front of you, what are you going to work with? And say to Self, "This is how I choose my life to manifest." Then you understand that you could choose this result . . . But if you look higher, you will see that there is a brighter result. Many of the prophets in the religions of the world speak of calamity and then healing and positiveness. It was the only way they had of expressing without technology, in a way that their own people could hear it. It was their way of saying, "You have the choice. You can have this calamity. It's right here, or you can move upwards of time and say, 'You know, I would really rather have this one. Doesn't it smell beautifully? Look at that radiant colour: How delicious, how delightful, how lush, how beautiful, how warm. I choose.' You know that as you choose, you are giving permission to others to make a similar choice. This is not about manipulating them. This is not about saying, "Oh God, if I make the wrong choice here, half the world is going to blow apart." It doesn't work like that. When you make your choice, you are then giving other people an understanding that behind this little door is something they may not have thought of; something they may have dreamed of; something they may have refused to dream of because they couldn't believe in it. But when you make your choice, you then display in front of them an expanded series of choices, and they have the opportunity to take whatever their choice will be, knowing that your choice, especially the positive, life-enhancing choices, vibrate a little more brilliantly in order to encourage attention but not require it. When you explore your intuition, when you understand that this can be something miraculous, when you understand and know that as intuition spreads throughout the world—and people begin to say, "This feels better. I had an understanding. It feels like someone dropped this spot into my mind, and I believe—I know—I will take it to heart and love it into existence"—when you accept, when you realize, that this intuitional energy demonstrates to you the connectedness of All of Life . . . It is not the trial and the trauma and the discombobulated energy of all of a sudden having great telepathy and having people go blink into your mind and hear you.

That is not the experience. The experience is a noticing. The experience is an awareness. The experience is the realization that not only those extremely close to you, but other people too are finishing your sentences, or they are starting to say something that you were thinking of, word for word for word, in your pattern. That is how telepathy will begin to show up. It is not about invasion of minds. It is about synchronicity. It is about choosing to be in contact and allow others to be in contact. It does not involve other people stomping through your mind as you walk down the street. This is about exploring potential. Your intuition becomes the means through which your Soul speaks to you; through which your Guides and Guardians speak to you; through which the Divine, God Goddess All That Is, speaks to you.

This is letting go of barriers that have been in place for thousands of years. Their usefulness is no longer valid. What has been called the still small voice within, will not be quite so still. It will be small in that it is not intrusive, but it will become much more clear. Instead of having to rely on the feeling of the body or a body sense, there will be a heart sense, and you will often simply know. Those individuals who have been encouraged and instructed to work with their intuition more, at this moment and in their past, are invited to be the vanguard, are invited to be the individuals who have that intuitional sense, strong and quiet within them. So that they can begin to teach others who all of a sudden say, "How did you know I was going to say exactly that? And when that happens, over, and over, and over, and over, and they move into panic, or they move into concern or move into questioning and know they need to explore this but don't know quite where to go, they will see you there; and you will say, "It is the natural thing. It is the way that things shall be. Congratulations, you are about to graduate."

This intuitional energy allows you to explore, not only emotions, but it allows you to explore intentions. It allows you the opportunity to see the results of your choices before they are made manifest, and therefore are less easy to dissolve or resolve. This extension from the heart by way of Divine connection allows you to expand in a graceful way, perhaps at first in a fun way. Don't you find this hilarious that we always have this connection.

It will come to those who are at peace and calm within Self, in order that they can share with others. This is about being calm and at peace within Self. There is no reason for panic. There is only a reason for understanding how beautifully, how fully, and how completely you are being accepted by The One and The All. You are on the first, the top, of their list of communication. Intuition—it brings Spirit in. It allows you to breathe with the heart and be connected, and it will expand. You will understand how connected your heart is to the heart of Gaia, and how connected your integrity is to the Creator of All Life Everywhere. It is another gift of love, and one of the most sacred and uplifting. As you move into this energy explore all the potentials, all the joys. They will assist you in manifestation.

# The Journey of Consultation—Archangel Uriel

Beautiful hearts, wonderful Souls, explorers indeed, how delightful that you are so passionate, and so curious, and so willing to look at not only the greatest potential for your Life but the possibility, little though it may seem at first, that excites you, that inspires you, that lifts you, from where you are to where you desire to be. This generation now living, from the grandparents to the parents, to the children, to the grandchildren, and to the newest ones, beginning their exploration of what Life can be like—this is a time in the world that has not yet been realized with regard to its potential, with regard to its understanding, and what is needed is consultation.

By opening yourself up beyond your opinion and saying, "I will hear what you have to say, and I will hear what this person has to say, and I will hear what is over here out, shall we say, in left field, and I will hear that as well and see, 'Can I make a beautiful life out of all of this.' So, there is interaction; there is consultation—between each of you. We find that as you go on with the circumstances of your Life, the way that it is so different from your parents, at times as confusing, and at times, indeed for women in particular, is especially empowering, as it was intended. But powerful women bring in powerful children, and the children always exceed the parents in times of evolution such as this is.

When you understand, that the parents who fight for their children and say, "This system needs to change," are creating situations in which the children take up that call and say, "I, as an individual, am perfect, and brilliant, and exactly the way I need to be to accomplish my purpose and will not be lumped together with everyone else." If you wish to perform a medical examination, know and understand that the words you are working with have changed. They no longer apply to the new generation because the new generation has not existed in a form in conformity to any of the generations that you have already explored, and we say as well, "Watch out because the generation following them is unique and individual as well." When you look at the potentials in your life, if you see limitation, if you see no choice, if you see disruption, and negativity, and carts before horses, you are seeing the old patterning. And that is an invitation; that is an inspiration—for you to go beyond that—to understand, "Yes," that there is value in uniqueness, to understand that robots are being created to take routine and sameness out of lives that have been shut down, locked down, by the requirement *to be the same as.*

When you accept your own unique beauty, and grace, and ability to understand, to know, to create, then you will feel like the individual working in a bank who stands up and looks across the whole floor of the executive level—The whole building can be seen, and every individual there has on black or navy—And then, this woman of independence, this woman of creativity, this woman of joy, looks down at herself and discovers that she has on a bright yellow tank-top, and bright yellow walking-shorts, and a jacket that is blue, and pink, and green, and yellow, and orange, and brilliant—and there is the reason to celebrate. The children—some of them now moving toward adulthood—can be very telepathic, can be either extremely positive in what they do or extremely negative in what they do, depending on the circumstances they have met, but each and every one of them says, "I am singular, one, unique, beautiful, perfect, needing to be heard," And if their life does not support that, then actions come forward where the system is shot into consulting within itself to say, "Why did this tragedy happen?"

And sometimes these investigations are not consultations. They are witch hunts: "Who can we blame? The child, the parent, the system, the school, the *this*, the *that*," instead of saying, "We are all one. Where did we fail this heart? Where did we stop listening?" When they begin to look from that point of view, when they take the first step and begin consultation—begin hearing these children, irrespective of their age, but hearing because they need a voice, hearing because there is potential there that is amazing, hearing simply because they are different—then the system will be able to work on behalf of the individual.

And then, limits will fly apart, and boxes will be exploded with passion, with love, with positiveness, instead of with pipe bombs. There are individuals who, because of their mental heritage, have heard only how inept they are; how wrong they are; how twisted they are; how out of sync they are. There are those who have the heritage of hatred and discrimination as part of their DNA, for DNA is not just a physical form. It originated in Spirit. It has intelligence. It has emotion, and it has a physical form so that it can be seen and explored in order to advance the humanness, the knowledge, of the Beings on the planet. Every single DNA strand has its own level of uniqueness. Yes, there are groupings. Yes, there are families et cetera, et cetera, but each individual's DNA is unique and becoming more so. And when you deal with the emotional DNA, you are dealing either with those who have been gifted with love, encouragement, support, strength where there seems to be none, compassion, and healing, or you are dealing with those who have only known hatred in all of its massive, destructive forms.

These are environmental, but they are also carried down the family line. There is an awareness; if a child is abused, it is because the father who abuses him was, in all likelihood, also abused. And so, when a man stands up and says, "I refuse to continue this energy, this potential, this DNA-driven action. I refuse to create children in order that this tendency stops here," and with that statement the line moves back, the energy moves back along to his father, and his grandfather, and further, and further back; so that that energy pattern can be healed; so that no one from that point forward—from that point in time and space, not in generation—from that point forward do not have to do the same actions, but it takes a strong individual. One who has explored for himself the consequences and the experience of being in that and said, "There's the line—shall not be crossed." Healing begins at that point; awareness begins at that point; consultation has occurred. He has consulted with his heart. He has consulted with his past, and he has consulted with those—in Love—with those in Spirit who understand what his needs are, who understand what his choice is. And then, by the Grace of Creation, when this individual has children brought into his Life experience, he has moved from that point of release and worked on healing, and it is a different man with a different genetic heritage that greets these children—with the result that healing occurs for all parties involved—Yes—because of the spiritual aspect of the DNA energy flow.

DNA in certain respects can be changed, not yet on the physical realm because there is still a need for the stability of physical DNA. But most definitely the spiritual guidance, the spiritual patterning, the spiritual evolvement, and uplifting energy of spiritual DNA affects the mental, and it affects the emotional—and so the intention of causing no harm, wrapped up with the passion that says, "It stops here." This is never an action to go against your ancestry; however, you view it to be. This is never an action that occurs in a quiet way. It does not occur in a blasé or detached way.

This is where compassion, intensity, and the-right-use-of-energy come together so that the shift can occur. And, it always comes through the intervention, one might say, the injection into Life, of spiritual DNA that says, "Change the vibration," and this type of change can only be a change for positiveness.

Negativity does not have access to spiritual DNA. It is simply unable to conceive, and; therefore, unable to manifest, that form of contact or consultation. When the heart and the higher intention come together, there is a result that goes beyond regulations, that goes beyond limitations, that goes beyond certain belief systems. The children in educational facilities have created great change, but it is not enough; and so, the shift of the energy, and the passion, and the understanding, and the conceptualization of new ideas is part of the next stage of healing the schools, of teaching the teachers, of focusing on the needs of the few or the one, in order that individuals understand and know that there is value there—that it is not always the many, the perceived majority, that runs the planet, or runs the show, or runs the school system, but rather that individuality is sacred and deserves support.

If Leonardo da Vinci had been forced to use his right hand, would he have been able to access all that knowledge, all that creativity, all that curiosity, that lay within this great Soul? You could indeed say, "Being left-handed he was always in his right brain." But if there had been the rigidity in the learning systems then that is present in the learning systems now, history itself could have been quite different. We applaud that certain higher systems of learning such as colleges and universities are seeking to expand their curricula, in order that what is of interest and benefit to more, and more, and more individuals can be offered. It is a sadness to us that only certain school systems are able to go beyond their outlines.

And understand that Life can be taught in many different ways . . . That there are individuals, because of their orientation into life—and this is not a condemnation, this is an individualization—do better if they can speak what they need to say—have it recorded and printed out—rather than having to struggle with remembering the shape of every letter, every time . . . A situation that says you must be in that seat, when the individual strength in learning, and remembering, and locking information into the mind goes through the physical self, and that writing or that walking are the way this individual learns. It is coming, but it is far too slow. It is far too slow indeed; nonetheless, the shift continues. Those individuals who grew up with parents saying, "You have to listen to your teacher. Don't come crying to me if your teacher said, 'That's it!'" and now, they, as parents, are saying, "I know my child. This is not logical. This makes no sense. This is not the way this child is," and you may think with the matter of a few hours, or days, or weeks of occasional interaction that you know this child; you may think that because you are an adult, you have the right to have this child expose himself by telling you intimate things about himself or even things that you consider to be casual ways of connecting with the child—does not give you the right always to know and get inside this child's barriers! Your authority gives you no rights! Your respect, and your interest, and your connection with this child—by consulting with him or her, by being empathetic and connected—that is what works! Your title means nothing. And so, you will find that as things continue more and more schools will be teaching the unusual until the point that such schools as the Waldorf system, and the Montessori system, and other systems of creativity and individuality begin to proliferate, and as more and more children consult with their parents to say, "This is the school I want to go. This is the learning I want to have." So shall the system change because the parents are now on the side of the child and not on the side of the teacher. Teachers often get caught up in their authority and believe that that gives them the right or the opportunity to decide for sensitive children what their strengths are, what their failures are, without realizing the damage they do, and there are physicians who do similar things, and of course with the opportunity to medicate and speak to children in negative ways. Their ability to cause harm is even greater. These children are here on a mission. They manifest their lives, and they manifest their situations, for a higher purpose, to extend into the world the invitation to join them on a new adventure, to explore the future together, or to be left behind because they choose not to make that leap, and sometimes the result of that refusal can be extremely intense, and sometimes the consequences of that refusal leave the teacher wondering whatever happened to . . . and sometimes they find out.

They are shocked because they know that whatever result occurred, they didn't teach it, and if it is tragic, then they need to explore their own culpability, their own responsibility for the outcome, and if it is possible, and positive, and expansive, and going very much beyond what the teacher ever dreamed for this individual, then maybe they need to explore their non-involvement, and some will. Hopefully, most will. There are the children who bring chaos to systems that are rigid and locked-in because they must change; they must move; they must orient themselves in a different way if Life is to continue, and if Life is to become what it is intended and needs to be . . . these system-busters, Indigo they have been named, but they are indigo and opal. They are indigo because of who they see and what they see, and they are opal to assist them in taking the world and snapping some of its foundations because those foundations are weak and not life-enhancing. And then following them—the negative ones who have spread negative chaos, the positive ones who have spread positive chaos, by extending themselves beyond what the system is able to measure, by extending themselves in their intelligence, in their passion, in their results, beyond what has been believed possible—these systems are stretched to the breaking point and if they do not become flexible and stretch with these children, they will be broken because they are no longer of use.

The system that identifies a child's ability based on an intelligence level that is not measuring accurately—based on a flexibility level, a physical level, that has no reference to the individuality, and the determination, and the passion of the individual but simply says, "Well, you didn't do this, and you didn't do this, and he didn't do this, so therefore . . ."—they haven't looked at the broad spectrum of what they have done. And therefore, following these children are the healers, the individuals who will take all of that chaos, all of that broken-apart rigidity and release it so that healing, and peace, and love . . . so that acceptance and understanding that All Life is One Life, that there is only unity in great diversity.

It is a difficult system sometimes for the human mind to comprehend, but this is not about mind energy. This is about heart energy. This is about understanding that when one looks at a huge, fully-leafed oak tree that they are seeing the symbolism of diversity in oneness. They are also seeing the understanding that All Life is One Life. And so, these new children heal, expand, question, in order that those who are being questioned have the opportunity to expand themselves by searching out the answers, that they too can understand that coming to a certain stage or a certain age doesn't mean you know all you need to know, and these children empower others as they go about their work because wherever they go, sooner or later, the question comes up, "How do you do that?" And wherever they go, sooner or later, the question comes up, "How do you know that?" And then, Joy of Joys, sooner or later, the question comes up, "How could I do that?" And then begins an exploration in great passion, expansion, and evolution.

Each of you is open to possibilities beyond what has been up to this point in time. You are open to possibilities of great curiosity and great potential. That is the hope of the new world. There will be, indeed, great strides made, but only by those who choose to see the Light and look to extend it.

# The Search for Peace—Archangel Michael

Dearly Beloved, indeed, in this part we will discuss why. Why bother exploring? Why bother going within? Why bother with the consultation? Why bother with the intuition. The intuition will occur anyway. Why should you desire to work with this? It is because in the critical times, even now, where more negativity, anger, upset, all of these energies, show up in the city, show up in the neighborhood, show up across the world . . . All of these are cries of terror, and cries of hopelessness, and cries of power.

Where can we find the peace? "I don't believe in peace anymore. You're supposed to protect me. Look what has happened to me. Look what has happened to my child. Look what has happened to my life." All that these people want, all that Gaia wants, all that your Souls want, is peace, and how indeed can it be manifest?

As individuals understand and know that it is important for them to take responsibility for their own lives, many of them are being faced with the potential or the actuality of having to fight a battle in order for that to occur. There are those who say, "This advertising, this insurance company, this government has said, 'I need to be more involved with my healthcare,' and so I'm going to be involved. I'm going to explore that. I'm going to try and find out, why did this thing that this person over here has decided to apply to me as a label, why did this happen? And what can I do about it?"

There is a consultation with the imbalance or the illness, and you say, "All right, who are you in my Life? What is the symbol in my Life for this disturbance?" And then you say as well, sometimes having taken a breath or a step back—the symbol that comes forward—then you say, "Okay, I can understand that. Now wash that away and tell me what do you need from me in order that you can say, 'Good girl, you've learned your lesson. I'm outta here,' and you can go teach somebody else because now I have my energy in balance. I have my understanding at a clear and calm level," but the medical professions don't see it that way. They continue to want the authority.

Now, most of them indeed do so out of a desire to help other people. That is the vast majority, and we certainly honour that. The medical profession is still a noble one, misguided at times, but there are doctors coming forward, trained in the Western way, who walk around with acupuncture kits in their lab coats. So things are changing. They are shifting. They are becoming more beautiful, indeed.

Now, there are individuals who say "War is good for the economy. It stimulates this, this, this, this, this, and this." Yes, it is good for the economy until you realize what parts of the economy are being stimulated by this warring. It is no longer necessary for women to use a war, with men off somewhere, in order for them to get a step into the business world. That has been accomplished. Indeed, many women now are going off to do the fighting themselves. So what is it about war that helps the economy? It helps the military. It helps the weapons people. It does stimulate development of, shall we say, mapping techniques, stealth vehicles, other things of this nature, and some of these military techniques have a wonderful application in the civilian world—in search and rescue, GPS is wonderful. In traveling amongst these crowded city streets, GPS helps you find your destination without having to look at a map and squint your eyes at a house number, all the while supposedly being the driver.

There are many benefits that can come but what is the price of these benefits? What is the price of a land mine, and what is the price of a land mine that takes a child's leg? What is the price of a bullet, and what is the price of a bullet that takes a life, indeed?

The price of peace too can extend the economy. When individuals are living in an area of the world where they are not constantly keeping their ears open for any sound that might be a sound of danger; where they do not regularly rush down to the basement and hope that their home will not be so shattered overtop of them that they will be presumed dead and never found; when one can live in space where choice is expanded, where because there is a peace today, tomorrow, the next day, next week, next month, planning can come into play. Arts, for example, can be expanded, and the arts require many tools. Is that not assisting the economy? Dance, perhaps, consultations each with the other, conciliating, loving—

All of these also stimulate the economy, more quietly, more gently, much more long-term, because you are not killing off those who are going to buy your products. The ultimate in a war is that there will be one person left standing, theoretically one country left standing. But, we will tell you, ultimately carried to its end, there might be one person left standing. "Oh darn, that's not enough to make a genetic gene pool that will carry anything on." There is nothing of benefit in a war, period.

The goal of Life is to seek peace. When one is in a peace-full state, Life works. You have heard us say to you before, "If you desire more prosperity, set your intention and then go to call, different spelling—p-e-a-c-e—peace. If you desire a relationship, set your image, work with the energy, and then let it go so the Universe can bring it to you in peace. Peace is the tool through which any positive creation is manifested, and when peace is not in plentiful supply, when there is negativity and war and hitting back, et cetera, et cetera, et cetera, all around you, there is no peace.

Then, what you have chosen to create an image of in order to manifest takes much longer because that denser, harsher, harder energy surrounding the period of manifestation is slowed right down.

When you are at peace, when Life is worth living, when Life is a Joy to live, when Life indeed allows you opportunity, after opportunity, after invitation to pick up, and receive, and choose whatever you would have as a delight in your Life, as Joy magnificent in your Life, then you understand that peace is not about being bored, that peace is not about living in a slow energy because war is more stimulating. It is about a level of contentment and trust, a level of passion and compassion, where everything works, click-click. Will you get bored with that? As you wish, but we know from having seen elsewhere and from having seen in your Life, in other lifetimes, that peace gives you the opportunity to explore so much more than you have ever allowed yourself to explore; that it can be very exciting, very stimulating; that you can wake up every morning and say, "You know, today I want to do something different."

Each and every one of you has the intelligence, the capacity, and the availability of education to live Life in the fullest extent, as Leonardo da Vinci did. Yes, it is true, he made weapons of war for his patrons, but that is not what he is greatest known for. He is greatly known for his inventions. He is greatly known for his paintings. He is greatly known for his ability to take a risk and try something new in the hope that it would work. And even though it has been several hundreds of years since he lived—and the awareness is that the painting of The Last Supper is disintegrating; it has been for some time—nonetheless, that magnificence and that beauty is available even now.

The risk that he took in choosing a new medium and choosing new ways of creating that medium, still worked. He had the passion to go beyond the ordinary and let the stars and his dynamic mind guide him wherever they would lead. This is what peace can bring. This individual when not directly under the influence of his patron, would set himself apart so that he had the time, the opportunity, the inspiration, the passion, the delight, and the risk taking, and the creativity to go beyond where he was yesterday in order to discover where new he could be tomorrow, and each and every one of you has this ability. When you seek peace for yourself, it is an energy much greater—It is true—than the bubbling energy of Joy. It is also much more durable. It is not so emotionally attached. It is about serenity. It is about calm. It is about that inner quiet that is so powerful that all tension, all the stress, all imbalance, can be healed and brought back to balance simply by its presence. When peace is present with you, at the fullest degree that it can be, nothing is going to cause you trouble because you understand that peace is the creative point of All Life.

And if there is a situation where one you love is removed from your Life—at that point, instead of going into weeping and wailing, not for the person who has passed but for yourself—go into peace. Take a deep breath—relax. Allow yourself to feel that Beloved Presence about you. They do want to communicate. They want you to be at peace—your Guides, your Guardian Angels, your Soul, your High Self, the Divine, the Goddess—All wish you to be in that state of peace so that together you can explore the next stages of your Life, and connect to, and understand that nothing is ever lost, so long as it comes from the Heart of Love, with the radiance of compassion, with the well-filled glass of joy. When you seek peace, you see empowerment.

If you are all worried about something—flustered, anxious, tense, deadlines pushing at you—your ability to create the answers you need to meet those deadlines, to deal with that stress, is greatly impaired. Whenever you are worried about your finances, you cannot create more money because of that tension. Whenever you are upset about your relationship, you cannot create a better relationship because of the upset. Whenever you say, "I hate cooking," you cannot create food that is life-enhancing and uplifting—when you are in that state of I-hate-cooking. This is the secret of it. When you are at peace, and you calmly start the cycle again, giving away money, giving away love, giving away understanding to yourself, and healing, and compassion, then it all comes back to you, and it comes back to you multiplied because it is the only way it can return to you.

It is a law; another word for law is God. That is how strict and secure that rule of goes-around-comes-around-fully-multiplied is, and it is a sign of your unwillingness, your lack of peace to accept that, if what you give out is exactly what you get back. That law cannot be broken of what-goes-around-comes-around, but it can be barriered by you. So when you say, "Oh, I owe you a penny," and you pay a penny without allowing this other person to be generous and not worry about it, then what is happening is that you are interfering not only with the penny that you owed in your mind, but also with the generosity of this other individual and even more with the potential for both you and him to receive the bounty. It's still there. It hovers. It waits. And if that individual that you would have given the penny to says, "I accept," then they are moving out of that stream of that limitation.

Allow the Universe to be generous. Allow the Universe to invite you to go beyond where you are so that you can be in a much more expansive, beautiful, uplifting, positive, and peace-filled place. That's what you're here for. That's what this new energy is all about. It can be an amazing transition if you become peaceful and decide that that is so, but if you say, "I hate change . . . I always . . . et cetera, et cetera . . ." you know what we are about to say, the Universe will say, "As you wish," and it shall be yours.

But when you explore the understanding that peace is your natural state, that connection to all of Life is part of the bargain; when you understand that coming together to benefit even one individual is the most powerful healing, teaching tool you can have because it is not possible to heal only one—and yet at the same time, My Loves, that is all that you heal, The One—and as you heal The One, all segments, all part and particle, all leaves of the one tree, all are healed according to their ability to accept, to accept, to accept. My Loves, we leave you with this thought: Your exploration of life—your journey from the Divine through all experiences and back again to the Divine—is often likened to that journey energy: "What do I need to learn this time? My life is a journey. What is my path?"

All of these are words that say, "You are step-by-step moving from where you were to where you can be. Open yourself to greater possibilities." As Michelangelo said, The greatest tragedy for a man is to set himself a mediocre goal, and then reach it, for he will never have the drive, the energy, the enthusiasm, to set another goal and go higher.

This energy that has come into the world can be seen as higher—in actuality it is brighter; it is faster; it is more uplifting—but however it chooses to be seen, or you choose to see it so that it makes sense to you, is important. You cannot go back to who and what you were. You can try to sit cross legged on the floor with your arms folded and say, "I'm not playing." You will eventually be pushed across that floor. It won't be fun. Each of you has the spirit, the curiosity, the enthusiasm, to wonder, "What's on the next page? What's behind the next door?"

We invite you to come with us, My Loves, and explore . . .

# QUESTIONS AND ANSWERS

As is his habit during group sessions like these, the Archangel Michael took questions from the audience. During the Four Archangel presentations some questions were of a more personal nature than others. Those that were deemed to have information of value to many have been chosen to be presented with these discussions.

*Is the nature of The Divine to inspire one to teach or share Its Glory with those who may not be aware?*

It is, indeed, the inspiration or the request of The Divine that Its lovingness, Its care and concern for each individual, be shared, provided it is shared in such a manner that the person who is receiving the information or the understanding is left free to make their own choice or decision or response to that information.

The Divine is vast and exceedingly filled with variety. One cannot say that there is one path to The Divine. One cannot say there is one way only, for there are many paths to The Divine. Share what you know and understand as you are guided to do so; yes indeed, but allow that the person listening has the option and the opportunity to accept or decline to accept your point of view, your orientation.

As each individual shares what they know or shares their understanding, then both parties in the conversation gain a greater understanding of the perception of Divinity and thereby expand their understanding of that loving energy. Any individual must have the opportunity to say, "I agree, or I am uncertain, or I do not believe that belief." By allowing and inviting a response, each individual has the opportunity to expand their understanding of their own point of view.

It is not a matter of saying, "I know, and no one else does," because that is not The Way it is at all. The Divine is far more vast than any single, incarnated consciousness can comprehend, and, therefore, The Divine can also be more than what one person, at first, may know. Each of you is an expression of The Divine. So your perception of that expression, the way you see it moving in your life, is unique to you, and that is what needs to be shared. Is the question answered? [Yes] Excellent.

*How does one know their heart, mind, and Soul are at peace? Is the shift quite profound?*

And so, My Loves, we will say to you that there are conditions; there are circumstances where the shift is exceedingly profound, but, as a general rule, it is a matter of a quiet awareness that filters upward within you, to the point where you look at Life and you say . . .

Wait a minute. I've just realized, a few days ago, I would have felt this way. Last week I felt off balance, uncertain. I was having recurring meltdowns, one might say, but now, when I look within, when a circumstance comes to my attention, I'm not upset anymore. I just feel very quiet, very calm.

Now, we will say to you that, as an example, and this is written as a story, but it is a true event. In *Les Misérables* when Jean Val Jean found out that another ex-convict was being tried as himself—and he knew that he would have to leave the life that he had lived with honour and respect, as the mayor of the town in which he lived—that when he fought with himself overnight to discover, "Can I stay here? Can I continue to live my Life knowing that I am safe here, knowing that no one will ever come after me again because this guy is taking my place, even though he's not me? Can I do this?"

And he fought with his conscience, and he remembered, all of his life, the circumstances, since the Bishop gave him the candlesticks and the silver spoons—he knew that he had to go and do good. And that battle with the part of himself that wanted to be safe and the part of himself that knew he had to right a wrong that was about to be done; that battle caused his hair to turn completely white overnight, and that was the outer symbol of the inner struggle.

But when he came to the conclusion that all he could do was go to the court and say, "You have the wrong man. This is me. I am Jean Val Jean. This is the wrong man," and take whatever consequences, knowing that at that time there would be no Forgiveness for himself; nonetheless, he went, and he went with a peacefulness, and he went with a serenity, but he had to fight hard for that.

In that instance and in circumstances like that, when the shift is very profound, in and of itself, the peacefulness is very deep and very rich, but that is a profound shift that occurs when an individual is in a state of great healing, of great, intense transformation.

Most of the time the transformations that occur, the shifts that occur, are very quiet, and that is because it is already occurring deep within yourself, within your subconscious mind, and when the conscious mind becomes aware of it, it is as if it very quietly bubbles up to the surface and lays there, calm and serene, and the conscious mind says, "Oh, look what I've noticed. Isn't that cool? Isn't that good? Isn't that great?" The changes are no less profound because of their intensity, but, as a general rule, it is a quiet thing, indeed.

*What goes on in the minds of those who are not able to move on in Life because of depression, abuse, or staying in unhappy relationships? What might they be carrying or holding on to?*

An interesting question, indeed—those who are holding on to situations because of depression stay in their state because their fear has become so strong that they cannot imagine for themselves something different. It is as if they are at the bottom of a very deep pit, and they do not see any Light at the end of the tunnel, any guidance above them. It is as if their feeling is so intense that they cannot open themselves to perceiving a brighter way, a different way. One of the most difficult situations to be in is depression because you do not have the energy to move yourself out of it.

In the case of depression we strongly recommend, on a time-limited basis, not to be taken forever, but to have the guidance and the support of a compassionate consultant and to take medication to assist in stabilizing the person at a position that is less intense, so that they can begin to be open to possibility, and as they move out of the deeply depressed state, they can then gradually release themselves from the medicated state, in order to be able to learn, on a gradual basis, to deal with the feelings that, unmedicated, simply overwhelm them.

Abuse is a situation where terror or control is used as a tactic to keep individuals imprisoned. The very young [and the very old], of course, need assistance to protect them and to get them out of abusive situations. Those individuals, in particular—the focus is often on women and women with children—are often so brow-beaten, the term is, so inundated with negative situations about themselves, that they cannot conceive, they cannot believe, in themselves until they get to the point where they understand, the only way to save their children from what they have received, from re-creating this same condition, is to get the children out.

Very often individuals remove themselves from abusive situations for the sake of those that they can no longer protect, but often they have been wounded in their self-esteem and self-regard to the point where they believe that they are value-less. They believe the propaganda they are being handed. These individuals, very much, need the belief and the support, not only of the community, but the belief in themselves that they are worthwhile enough, to assist them in moving out of the situation.

It is a very sad thing when a person is so wounded in self-esteem that they will put themselves back in a situation because they believe they deserve nothing better. Certainly, writing to the angels[5] will assist in opening a shift in this pattern.

Those individuals who stay in unhappy relationships, we encourage to, at first, discuss, if it is possible to discuss, with their partner ways and means of creating the relationship as the greatest importance, that both of them are working together to create a magnificent relationship, but if one person is willing to work and the other is not, then we do not encourage individuals to stay in situations that are wounding, damaging, abusive, or unhappy for themselves. And so, therefore, we encourage, "Find love. Find self-respect. Move yourself out of where you are." Those individuals who are in holding patterns are often carrying karmic information, as well as this-Lifetime information, that they need to transcend, that they need to let go of, so that they can begin to strengthen themselves and move beyond these situations.

It is never appropriate to stay in a situation that causes you hurt—mental, physical, emotional, or spiritual—or puts you in any kind of danger, and even those who are deeply religious and who feel that, "What God has put together let no man put asunder."—need to understand that when one partner in a relationship hurts, or abuses, or transgresses, or creates unhappiness, in a relationship, that that person has already put the marriage or the partnership asunder, and so there is no violation on the part of the person escaping to a positive situation in Life. Very often, their karma is to give them the opportunity to go beyond where they are, and it is always a positive thing to encourage them to seek happiness.

---

[5] See Page 222, "Writing to the Guardian Angels," © Michel Green, 1997

*Was the number, "16 Lifetimes", taken randomly or specifically in the first part.*

And this was Gabriel speaking about being bitter for 16 Lifetimes. There are, of course, no accidents, and so there is a purpose. There is a reason behind the sixteen. The sixteen encourages *one*, the individual involved, the individual seeking peace within themselves, to create Love, beauty, centering (which is the *six*), to make that decision (which is also a part of the *six* vibration), to make a decision on behalf of Love in order to release themselves from the imprisonment of that many Lifetimes of bitterness. When the two are added together, this is a *seven* vibration, and *seven*, of course, is a spiritual orientation. The number was chosen in order to encourage individuals to make the choice for a positive outcome rather than imprisoning themselves in a situation that can be very stressful because the *seven* vibration, a spiritual Life, in a world where materialism and groundedness in the physical is the prevalent thought pattern, can be stressful, indeed. And so, it is encouraging a choice, by the one, to make the decision to choose Life, choose beauty, choose harmony, rather than experiencing devastation and stressfulness.

*How do I know which Angel is communicating with me?*

A wonderful question indeed—we would suggest that when the awareness comes forward that an Angel is communicating, that you say to this being, this vibration, "Who are you?" Angels coming from the Light are always very delighted to give their name, their vibration. Those who may not come from the Light often bring a feeling of, "Something's not quite right here," and we would strongly recommend that you pay attention to that. If you feel that the name that you are being given is inaccurate, then you say, "In the Name of the Christ, tell me who you are." That is an irresistible command, and they must then speak the Truth.

Even when you are familiar with those Angels who guide you—you have had ongoing and long-term communication—from time to time, it is appropriate to, shall we say, do a check. Ask for the ID, just to make sure that you have the energy that you believe you have.

*Please define the Council of Twelve. Who or what do they represent in each of us?*

Every Soul created has a Council of advisers or Higher Guidance. From time to time, these beings shift in their association with the Soul as the Soul progresses. These are always beings of very high evolvement who are interested in working with the individual to ensure that what is chosen for Life experiences are those experiences that will facilitate the growth of the individual. They tend to encourage a creative outlook and a very balanced situation.

It is happening more and more frequently that individuals are taking on comparatively intense Lifetimes in order to clear karma at a very quick level, and that is because many Souls are under the understanding—and the true understanding—that the population of the planet will be diminished over the course of the next two hundred odd years, and; therefore, there will be less opportunity for Souls wishing to incarnate to have that opportunity. Many of them are, therefore, asking for a greater intensity of Life so that their progress may continue. As some of you know, those beings who do not incarnate on the physical plane do progress, but their progression takes much, much longer. This school here, this experience here, facilitates the Soul's growth. Having said that, the Council of Twelve can also be represented symbolically by the twelve archetypes that Carolyn Myss talks about in her book *Sacred Contracts*, and if you wish to understand some of the qualities and some of the vibratory resources that you have, you could go through this material, and it will assist you in understanding some of the talents, abilities, and challenges that you have brought with you as symbolic representations of what you can accomplish in your Life.

The Council of Twelve are advisers. Sometimes, they make recommendations that certain circumstances do not occur, but all of the choices that the individual about to incarnate and their council come up with needs to be approved by the Most High before that incarnation can take place. In this way, no individual brings into creation for themselves more than they can handle, even those with intensity in their lives, such as many Scorpio people, but then, of course, all of you have Scorpio somewhere in your experience.

*Is it true that if you forgive someone on this plane or in this Lifetime, you no longer carry the energy or the charge into the next Lifetime?*

Absolutely it is true. Once you have forgiven them—whether they choose to accept that Forgiveness, whether they choose to act on that Forgiveness, whether they choose to forgive you in turn, is immaterial—by forgiving them, you have moved beyond that vibration. You have moved beyond the necessity for that experience, and when you return in Life, even if they incarnate with you side-by-side, the two of you will not be drawn together. The two of you will have no reason to come together again, and so it goes to completion. If they have not forgiven you, then they will meet with someone of similar vibration to themselves who will give them a harder lesson through which to learn Forgiveness, indeed, and that is why we, shall we say, sometimes tend to nag on this subject, because it makes it much easier for you in your next Life if you have already forgiven. The make-up tests are no fun, indeed.

*How can we begin to create miracles, for example, spontaneous healing or instantaneous money, et cetera?*

The first thing—perhaps the most difficult, but we would hope not—is to believe that it is possible, to train your heart and mind to understand that it is only your belief, that it takes a period of time for something to manifest. Time is a man-made thing. It does not truly exist. At first, it will be necessary for you to choose an idea, fall in love with that idea so it becomes an ideal, it becomes a goal, and then after a suitable period of gestation, it becomes real in your life. So at first that process occurs very slowly and for many of you that period of gestation is the most difficult part, but we will say this:

> By affirming on the regular and frequent basis to yourself that, 'Life and all of my experiences are miraculous, that The Divine works through me in an amazing and miraculous manner to bring me all of my needs and all of my desires as I become aware of them, and I am open to receive miracles in a positive, gentle, and loving manner,' these are ways indeed of working with that energy, of working with that instantaneous manifestation.

It is absolutely possible for every individual hearing my words to create this. It is your belief or rather your disbelief that presents a block. Know that your income, for example, has nothing to do with the price you charge or the work that you do. It is simply a response from the Universe for all that you have given away in life. So when you are having difficulty with money, for example, when you want to hold onto what you have tightly, and understand that prevents any more from coming in to you; when you are at that state of tension give a little money—no strings attached—just give a little away.

When you come to the point where you are calm about money, it begins to move for you very, very positively. In this vein we would recommend to you a book by Stuart Wilde called *Miracles*. It will give you further insight.

*Why does it feel arrogant to think of myself as MAGNIFICENT?*

How beautiful that it is in all capitals—THE MAGNIFICENT

*How can I overcome this?*

Dear and Wonderful Ones, it is a misuse of teaching that has brought to you the understanding that it is arrogant, self-centered, to think of you as more than or what some would say, "better than," another individual. Every being incarnated, every being in this realm of Spirit, is magnificent; that is, in essence, who they are. By accepting this and going beyond what society has said, it is not a matter of being arrogant; it is a matter of overriding the fear and the judgmentalism that you have been brought up with, this lifetime and others. By identifying yourself as Magnificent, many people will interpret that as being "better than", but when you identify yourself as Magnificent, you are linking yourself and acknowledging that the Magnificence of creativity, that the magnificence of All That Is, is who you are. By simply allowing yourself on a regular basis to say the word *Magnificent*—and pull it into the heart of you, and then allowing that energy to flow out and fill every cell of who you are—this allows you to understand and this allows you to overcome any judgment that would interfere with the Truth of who you are. At first, it will be appropriate for you to keep this quietly to self until you are so in tune with the understanding of yourself as Magnificent that what another person says no longer has an effect on you. Part of this has to do with the ancient feeling of being insecure if you step outside of your place, your cast, your role. It is more than time for this energy to be cleared from you so that you can move into the Truth of who you are.

*How do we begin to clear out residual memories and experiences, the ones holding us back?*

The good news is it does not need to be difficult, and we hope that that inspires hope within you. The individuals who find those negative memories that keep cropping up and haunting them are those individuals of very high sensitivity, who have been wounded by these old memories, by these experiences, traumatized at a very deep level. And so the memory keeps coming forward, in part, because these individuals not only are highly sensitive but are also exceedingly intelligent, so much so that it is difficult to sublimate a memory if it has a strong energy about it, coupling that with the fact that the human creature has a tendency to remember negative situations for a much longer period of time and remember the negativity to a greater depth of painfulness as compared to good things that, even though they may be exceedingly joyous, [they] do not have the intensity of energy and are not remembered for as long a period of time. So having combined all of these factors, it makes it appear to be more difficult to rid yourself of these.

We would recommend two actions: First of all, that when a memory comes forward that is not a pleasant or positive one, ask your Guides and Guardians to come in and fade it on the page of your memory. First of all though, we would suggest that you take a look at that memory and say, "What in there could you possibly have for me that allows me to discover the silver lining?" Every experience has a silver lining for you. Some of them are buried so deep and filled with energy from yourself and from the experience, that it may feel like slogging through muck and mire in order to get to it, but, nonetheless, it is there. It is much more effective for you to simply say, "Okay, Memory, here you are. You've been haunting me for a long time; I'm getting tired of this. What do you have to teach me? I want it clean, clear, and in a positive manner."

And when you understand—that in a great many circumstances it has taught you how to survive; it has taught you strength; it has taught you to release from your experience, from your memory, other people's points of view or value, or devaluing, of you; it has taught you that your opinion, your experience, your understanding, of the beauty, and the dynamic, and the wondrousness of yourself counts more than what anyone else might have done to pound something different into you.

> It has given you—it is intended to give you—that strength to say, "I choose. I choose my life, and my choice says, 'This is not who I am. It wasn't then, and it's certainly not now.' Okay, got the lesson, thank you, you're dismissed. Go and find someone else to teach. Thanks for helping my journey."

And they are released; they no longer have any power over you. They no longer have a way or a means of holding that—hooking you—because you have released them. You have said, "Thank you," to them, and so they are gone. And not only that but having come to a state where you can understand the benefit that that traumatic situation had for you, you begin to dissolve all the negativity from this point forward back to that original situation. The understanding, the experience, will still be there, but its power to be of harm to you is gone.

All that energy is dissolved, and it simply becomes a fact of something that once happened, but you have gone forward from it; you have healed from it. Life is more positive, and you don't even have to go there anymore. It just sits there on a bookcase gathering dust, a fact among other facts, but nothing that can touch you any longer. Those circumstances that keep coming up to haunt you have not yet fulfilled their purpose. You have not understood fully what they were meant to teach you. When you do . . . gone.

*I believe a message is trying to come through to me through sensation at the left knee and left arm. Can you give any insight?*

Congratulations on your perception. Indeed, we find that the energy that is occurring here is an awakening and an awareness of Divine, Feminine Energy. Feminine energy, as you may be aware, is predominantly left-sided. It is the receiving energy; it is energy moving in. Masculine energy, of course, is outward moving energy and therefore right-sided. Having said that, we find that there is an encouragement for an enhancement in Goddess energy and Goddess awareness. To be walking on the path of The Divine Feminine is part of the message that is coming through the left knee, to be open to valuing self and loving self through the receiving and the holding in a gentle, positive manner of The Divine, Feminine energy, energy that is available for each individual. This is not about gender; this is about creativity; this is about co-operation. This is about the cycles of energy and the circles of energy, and this is about being in Life in order to bring every individual to a level, a peer level, a level of harmony, a level of justice, when they are in your presence. We find as well and would certainly recommend—perhaps each of you might wish to search out those energies that resonate for you—but we will recommend three books: (Pick them up as you choose) *Goddesses in Every Woman, Gods in Every Man, Goddesses in Older Women*. Whichever of these you are drawn to are the ones that have further information for you at this time, but we will say to you that as you continue through life, this information will become important to your work, and having the opportunity to read all of them so that you can assist in service to other individuals regardless of gender, will be a highly recommended practice that we offer to you. The author is Jean Shinoda Bolen, and we certainly recommend this for you. Thank you for pointing out the message that needed to come through.

*What is fearlessness?*

And that is an amazingly wonderful question. It is a question of *acting* without fear. It is not a matter of being without fear, but it is a matter of choosing to transcend that fear, to remind your fear that it is intended to be your servant, not your master; that it has a job to do in giving you warnings, not dictates; and when you lessen your fear, it becomes your servant again. It becomes your advisor again which is its role. And so you say to it, "Old and dear friend tell me what you perceive, and I will take it under advisement, and in the meantime rest," and when you move yourself into that energy that fear has an opinion in your life, as do other energies around you, but understand and know that you have the only vote.

You are the one who makes the choice, and if you give up your power to your fear, then that is enhancing and upgrading your fear to master, and it is not a wonderful master. When you lessen the energy of fear, that is what it means, fear-less. When you look at that and know that you can come to a state of fearing less by giving your circumstance over to the Divine, by empowering yourself, by saying to those who guide and guard you, "In this situation, I am open to your recommendations. I am open to your guidance." Now, remember clearly, guidance is about offering advice and pointing out a direction. It is not about planting hands in your back and pushing you. Guidance is not an order. It is not a means of taking away your power, and that is what we do. We make suggestions. We make recommendations. We offer you expanded options, and then it is up to you. When you move into a state where you fear-less, it is because you are loving more. Does this answer the question? (Yes). Excellent.

*Can you advise us how to know when to (1) have the courage to step towards our desire, and (2) when to have the courage to surrender?*

Excellent indeed, you do both at the same time. By identifying what you desire, by observing it, and focusing on it, and feeling the emotion of it, and moving yourself into that vibratory state, and yet saying . . .

> This is what I passionately want. This is where my focus is. This is where my energy is. If it is for my highest good, I accept. If it is not, then I know and understand that something better is on its way, and I release conditions.

When you surrender, what you are doing is not giving up; what you are doing at that point is giving the entire situation over to the Divine and letting the Divine look after it. If, for example, you wanted a relationship that was beautiful and life-enhancing, that made you feel very loved, very supported, very cherished, and that gave you the inspiration and the desire to do that for the other individual, a magical relationship that other people would say, "I want that when I grow up," and you focus on that and you strongly, strongly desire that. When you surrender, you say . . .

> Okay God, this is my vision, and I am passionately involved with it. I can almost feel it, but I am giving you all of this. I trust and know that you will take care of it in the very best way possible, and you let it go.

And when a friend of yours says, "Aren't you ever going to get into a relationship," and fear rises up within you, you say . . .

> Not my job, I gave that to God. God is looking after it. I don't have to worry about it, not my job. I am open to receive it, and I am focusing. I am reminding. I am becoming very, very clear on what it is that I want.

It is why we say write your vision down because your mind tends to change things and move things around and leave one thing out and add something else in, but if you have your vision written down, it is a precise instrument that you could focus on, and then the Universal Mind knows clearly what it is that you want, rather than having this blurry wish. So, the two are the same. You do the two together. When you choose your desire, when your desire comes knocking at your heart, and when it won't give up, when it keeps coming to your attention, when you say, "Well yeah, maybe, okay," and you go off and do something else and circumstances bring you back to this being in front of your face again, when it keeps reminding you, it is saying, "I want to be part of your life. Choose me." And when you agree to do that, it is wonderful. But when you accept that the Divine knows the best way how it can happen, that is the point of surrender, giving over, not giving up, giving over, so that the Divine can create it for you in the best and most beautiful way possible. The answer is: You do both.

*This talk feels so serious. Can you please say something about courage and playfulness and fun? Sometimes being brave is fun.*

How delightful, how delightful indeed, courage is a little child learning to walk, and she stands up with one hand on the table and there in front of her the smiling, laughing face of one she loves, and she knows she wants to go there, but she knows also she needs to let go of her support in order to be there, and so she does. She reaches out, and reaches out, as far as her little arm will let her go, and then, oh, takes that courage, and takes that step, and takes another step, and then runs and oohh to be caught up laughing, joyful, and then this small little face claps her hands because she has been brave. She has taken that risk, and she has succeeded because that is where her focus was.

Courage sometimes is like Leo Buscaglia has said many times, Having the courage to do things in a different way, in an unexpected way, can give you so much leeway for joyful behaviour. This was an amazing Soul who would gather all the leaves in his yard in the fall, and gather them up into a big pile, and then, with neighbours watching and going, "That crazy Buscaglia," he would charge into the leaves and scatter them everywhere because it was fun to do.

And so, that takes courage because it is outside the expectations that others have for you or for their own lives, but by allowing yourself to be crazy-courageous, by allowing yourself to go out and stomp through puddles and look up in the rain, and stick your tongue out, and drink the snowflakes that land on your tongue, and never give a thought for acid rain because that is a fear-based action, for going out on a summer's day with your beloved and starting a snowball fight, knowing that he's likely to get you smoosh in the face, but if you hit him first, you win this year, and there is always next year for him to have a chance back.

Courage is about finding the bravery to be true to the spirit of fun within you, without judgment and without allowing the influence of other people's opinions to limit you. Courage is about looking at your Life and saying, "Okay, for the next year what would make me happy? What would I love to do? Where would I love to be? What would be the most fun?" We take life, indeed, far too seriously, and so giving yourself an opportunity, every single week if not every single day, to do something that is fun, for that reason and no other, can be an exhilarating experience, but it does mean that you will go outside the box of expectation that others have built around you, and some will think you're absolutely crazy, and others will think that you're totally out of your mind, and others will think that you are so full of yourself that they don't know you anymore, and they don't want to know you anymore. So many of you are filled with the feeling that you must live up to other people's expectations rather than your own that you put limits on your Joy. It does, indeed, take a great deal of courage to tear the lid off that box and allow who you would like to try being to come forward. Every month we make the recommendation, ask yourself . . .

What would I love to do because it's out of the ordinary, it's fun—I haven't done it for at least thirty days—It's going to shock some people and jar their preserves, but that is fine.

Sometimes people need a good shake-up so that they can learn to laugh at the world.

I'm quite willing to be God's agent for fun at some point in this month. What can I do that's going to make me laugh and other people laugh?

And as you begin this process, some of you will say . . .

Okay, I'm quite willing to let my Inner Child out and be free, and be silly, and have fun, and giggle until my sides ache, just because it's a good day to giggle until my sides ache, but I'm not quite sure I can do it just yet.

    Find an accomplice. You want to go to a "children's movie", borrow a child. Go there. Sit there, the two of you with your feet up on the seat in front of you and gorge on popcorn, and red licorice, and pop until you can hardly wait for the end of the movie so that you can get to the bathroom, but laugh and giggle and enjoy, simply because that is what you are here to do. Put it on your calendar. The seriousness of your life, My Loves, will gobble that up if you don't make it a date with yourself. Red ink, so it can't be erased and can't be ignored. Life is meant to be fun, and it takes courage. It takes that heart-filled exuberance to make it so.
    You are the captain of the ship of your own lives. Like Picard sitting in the command chair, you are the one who can "Make it so." Laugh well, and your health is enhanced. Laugh uproariously, and your mental state is sparkling and can see so many more options. We remind you that although Love is the basis for All Life Everywhere, it is the most common vibration in the realm of Spirit. We would remind you that Laughter is the second most common vibration, and many of you are down on your quota.
    Dear Hearts, raise your glasses to your Life. Salute it. Celebrate it, and laugh as you drink it down. It is a recipe for good health, indeed. We are delighted at your attendance and, in particular, at your questions. The root cause of your life, the reason you incarnated, not only this lifetime but others, is to transcend the experiences that tend to push you off balance, to

find a reason to be your own person, in joy, in delight, in laughter, to move beyond the pain that Life has been and discover that every challenge has a silver lining. It is a guarantee.

What you need to do is to pick the fluff and the disguise off that challenge in order to find the benefit for you, the silver lining, the fun point, and if it appears that you are getting to the very heart of it, and there is no fun point, then make up some form of positiveness, of joy, of laughter. Create something from that. Take several pages in a sketchbook and diagram where you started with this episode and keep going, layer by layer by layer, until you can come to that smooth, soft, serene place of release that is at the end of every difficult situation. You are a very courageous individual. This lifetime was not required of you, in particular of the intensity, but you have chosen this, and you never are allowed to bring in more than you can bear.

By understanding that each time you go through a challenge, the next one is intended to become easier, and move into that level of awareness. So shall it be—Our Blessings to each of you, My Loves. Go in laughter.

# Writing to the Guardian Angels

Writing to the Guardian Angels can be a very effective way of enlisting their support in any venture in your life. When you feel most uncertain, taking the time to impress your desire on the Universal Mind by writing it not only helps you become clear about what you really want but also helps you focus on the positive.

Angels and Guides are unable to intervene in our lives spontaneously because of our Free Will. Since the Angels need to be asked to help us, this is a special way of asking that is clear, focussed and obviously important enough to commit to the number of days required for the process.

## *The Protocol*:

Each day [evening usually works best] for 15 days, you write a *brief* note to your Guardian Angel asking for the result you desire.

It is not necessary for you to know your Guardian Angel's name. Simply address your note, "To My Guardian Angel" or "To the Guardian Angel of _____ and My Guardian Angel" when your writing concerns situations or others. You can write to the Guardian Angel of a company, government or country, if desired.

At the end of the 15 days, burn all the letters to allow the energy to be released in a dynamic way.

## *Additional Notes*:

Keep these writings to yourself. This is a very sensitive instrument that sets a more positive energy in motion but it can be diminished by disbelief. After all, the angels often like to work behind the scenes.

If you start the writing and then stop for longer than a day, then you will have to start all over again. And if you notice a change occurring before the end of the 15 days [the ancient number of completion], it is important to finish the writing otherwise, the energy will fade and dissipate.

Most importantly, you will find this works well when you leave your judgement aside and let the angels do what's best. Asking for the creation of a positive relationship between yourself and another, for example, is what these letters were designed for—rather than asking that the other person "get fixed."

It is an excellent practise to include a word of gratitude for the blessing in each note.